YOUR CHURCH CAN COME Alive

YOUR CHURCH CAN COME Alive

Strategies for church leaders

by Rowland Croucher

The Joint Board of Christian Education
Melbourne

Published by
THE JOINT BOARD OF CHRISTIAN EDUCATION
Second Floor, 10 Queen Street, Melbourne 3000, Australia

YOUR CHURCH CAN COME ALIVE

Copyright © Rowland Croucher 1991

This publication is copyright. Other than for the purposes and subject to the conditions prescribed under the Copyright Act, no part of it may in any form or by any means (electronic, mechanical, microcopying, photocopying, recording or otherwise) be reproduced, stored in a retrieval system or transmitted without prior written permission from the publisher.

Scripture quotations are from The GOOD NEWS BIBLE — Old Testament: Copyright © American Bible Society 1976: New Testament: Copyright © American Bible Society 1966, 1971, 1976.

National Library of Australia
    Cataloguing-in-Publication entry.

Croucher, Rowland.

Your church can come alive.

Bibliography.
ISBN 0 85819 809 6.

1. Pastoral theology. 2. Christian leadership. I. Joint Board of Christian Education. II. Title.

253

First printed 1991

Cover concept by Alfred Hickey
Design by Kelvin Young
Typeset by Bookset Pty Ltd in Cheltenham book
Printed by Shannon Press Pty Ltd

JB91/2972

Contents

Preface   7

Foreword   8

1. The church as a critic of culture   13
2. Towards an evangelistic lifestyle   15
3. Mature churches take risks   18
4. Be evangelical or perish!   21
5. Communicate!   23
6. Your cleverness isn't enough, however   26
7. The disease of nominalism   30
8. Penitence and holiness   34
9. Interdependence: a sign of maturity   36
10. The best committees are committees of one! (or: was that meeting really necessary?)   39
11. Barnabas the Encourager: may his tribe increase   44
12. The gift of sanctified permissiveness   48
13. Get with it: be committed!   51
14. Leaders who love goodness   54
15. How to be filled with the Holy Spirit   57
16. The (corporate) just shall live by faith   60
17. Team ministries   63
18. Leadership selection: move with the movers!   68
19. The teaching ministry of the church   72
20. Congregational participation in worship   79

21.	Listen to the prophets	84
22.	Compassion and mercy	87
23.	Financial generosity	91
24.	Who's in charge?	98
25.	Do your people know their spiritual gifts?	101
26.	Affirming diversity	104
27.	Social justice: get involved!	106
28.	Worship: who's the audience?	109
29.	Fasting is healthy!	112
30.	On listening to the Holy Spirit	114
31.	Ministry as empowerment	116
32.	Christians who pray together	120
33.	Commissioning for ministry	125
34.	The world is your parish	127

Postscript
Live in hope: your church can come alive!   130

Appendix
In search of pastoral excellence: a ministry empowerment questionnaire   133

Preface

This small book (together with a 4½ hour videotape and worksheets)* is meant to serve as a training manual for pastors and church leaders. Its aim is to familiarise elders, deacons, church wardens and other leaders in a local church with ideas about the theology of and leadership in the church which are current in the disciplines of Biblical and Practical Theology. Throughout the world there are many ordinary Christians — plumbers, teachers, homemakers, doctors or whatever — who, following a vote in a church meeting, are 'pitchforked' into leadership in their church without any prior training.

Here we attempt to answer, albeit very briefly, most of their questions. It's a sort of 'everything you always wanted to know about church leadership but were afraid to ask' book.

Thanks are due to World Vision of Australia, whose commitment to 'Leadership Enhancement' allowed this project to be birthed and come to its present adolescent phase (I need your ideas, comments and feedback to bring it to maturity!); to many churches and pastors' conferences who gave these ideas an airing; to Grace Thomlinson, Anne Bridgman, Flo Sinclair, Anne Carroll and our daughter Karen McPhie, for help with administration and typing; to John Springall who ensured the computer stayed cooperative; and to Jan, Amanda and Lindy, for their patience in allowing their husband and father to spend a third of his time on the road, in the air, in many conferences and in many books!

Have fun! May this study enable you to see more clearly the possibilities in your congregation!

Shalom!

Rowland Croucher

---

* Available for $95 Australian, from the Leadership Enhancement Department, World Vision of Australia, Box 399C, Melbourne, Australia, 3001 or from Rowland Croucher, John Mark Ministries, 7 Bangor Court, Heathmont, Australia, 3135.

Foreword

The worst evils in the world are not done by evil persons; the worst evils in the world are done by good persons who do not know that they are not doing good.

Reinhold Niebuhr

Twenty years ago I had two conversations I will never forget. A couple of university students told me why they loved Jesus but hated the church. One was a 'Jesus freak', dressed like a hippie, and was told by a man in a suit at the church door he couldn't come in unless he was 'respectable'. 'I wonder what he would have told John the Baptist?' this serious young man asked. The other student had got in, but it was his first and only visit to a church service. He was sincerely searching for God, but 'so much hocus-pocus went on in there that I couldn't follow. It was all dead. I never went back'.

As an 'ordained' 'minister' (I'll explain the 'quotes' later) working full-time with the Inter-Varsity Fellowship, those comments led to two resolves: first, to do some serious research. A Master's degree in Social Psychology would study the issue of change in the church. Second, to put this research into practice, I would make myself available to a parish to see if the theory worked.

'It was all dead' that disillusioned student told me. Who or what is killing so many churches? That question can be answered many ways. The 'evil one' as Jesus called the Devil, is masterminding a cosmic conspiracy to keep the church divided and weak. Outdated traditions kill churches when they become irrelevant. It is also a question of power: instead of empowering the church's future leaders, many pastors are, perhaps unintentionally, creating systems of dependency to enhance their authority and ensure their survival. A church can be ancient or modern, sepulchral or noisy, 'liturgical' or 'free', evangelical or liberal, hell-fire preachin' fundamentalist or mainline charismatic, tongues-speaking Pentecostal or a social-action Uniting Church — I have met diseased and dying churches in all these categories. In their death-throes some are noisier than others!

Ultimately it comes down to the confusion of ends and means. The main thesis of this book is that worship, community, formation and mission are the four (and the only four) ends for which the church exists. The means whereby these ends are reached include leadership, money, buildings, music, programs, constitutions, committees, etc. When 'means' and 'ends' become confused or the time, attention and importance given to 'means' outweighs that devoted to the church's 'ends' the church becomes sick and often, after a generation or two, dies.

Worship is everything the people of God do for God's glory: so 'gathered' worship ought to be closely tied to worship in the world. **Community** is the meeting of spiritual gifts and human needs. **Formation** is the process whereby the Word of God is applied to the heart and mind of the child of God so that she or he becomes more like the Son of God. **Mission** is everything the church does in the world, involving compassion for the oppressed (justice), the hurting (mercy) and the lost (evangelism).

So church renewal is the process whereby church people, systems and structures receive new life, meaning and power. Ministry renewal is the process whereby pastors and leaders move from an organisational-maintenance mode of leadership to one of empowering the whole church for ministry.

Although produced Down Under, these principles are, I believe, universal. They have been forged in pastors' and church leaders' conferences in a dozen countries. Just about every Christian denomination you can think of was represented at these seminars.

I love the church. But I'm a critical lover (or a loving critic!). For the past eight years I have been a consultant with pastors and their co-leaders; I have spent much of my time thinking, writing and speaking about the church.

Before that, two sets of contrasting experiences served as 'grist' for much of this material. First, I had two rewarding pastorates: Narwee Baptist Church in Sydney, and the Blackburn Baptist Church in Melbourne. My thanks to the members of these congregations for their patience with this sometimes provocative pastor! The Narwee church added two extra staff members while their 'senior' pastor was still a part-time theological student; the missionary giving rose two thousand per cent; several young people left for Bible and theological colleges and full-time missionary service. The Blackburn experience began with one and one-third staff: I was the 'one', my secretary the 'third'! In just five years our accountant was writing salary cheques for twenty-five people!

But something happened in Canada in 1981-2 that was even more profound. The Narwee-Blackburn episodes had produced a somewhat unfeeling triumphalism: 'We did it — you can too, if you're smart!' What arrogant nonsense! Would Jeremiah have done it our way? After nine months of a pastorate in Canada, I resigned. The details aren't important; let's say it was a 'mutual mismatch of expectations and reality'. Then followed a year of doubt, depression, study (at Fuller Theological Seminary), prayer, reflection and healing.

The Easter event includes everything from Gethsemane to resurrection; the church ever since has re-enacted in its life and sacraments this counterpointing of darkness and light, pain and glory. Luke's stories in Acts are somewhat triumphalistic — that's all right, provided you also study the suffering churches in Peter's epistles and John's Revelation. In Europe, and to some extent in Britain, I experience a pervasive though sophisticated gloom in the church; in the US, a lot of superficial hype. A healthy church won't follow either pattern.

I believe many of the world's greatest churches have yet to be born; most of them won't be large or Western. I have nothing against large congregations — I have been privileged to pastor a couple. I believe, however, that the pursuit of growth-goals rather than spiritual health is dangerous and many evangelical pastors have been seduced by uncritically swallowing a 'church growth' paradigm for their church's life. Almost every week I meet disillusioned pastors who have fallen for this illusory model.

The church of Jesus Christ is glorious, not because it's perfect but because it was 'died for' and is being redeemed. Your church can be healthy, but it will only 'come alive' if the pastor and leaders and people are willing to pay the price. All birthing is painful, all growth is costly. But the experience of acceptance, joy and fruitfulness in a mature, loving church is something only heaven will surpass. Let us, with the help of the Lord of the church, create colonies of heaven in our churches!
(*Video tape 1: 'Introduction' expands on the ideas suggested so far.*)

Case study of a dynamic church

In this book, we'll use the church at Antioch in Syria to help us understand how a church comes alive. We know more about this church than any other in apostolic times. Luke, the author of Acts seems to offer it as a model for churches everywhere: a 'prototype' for the local church of any Christian denomination in any culture, at any time.

It was a balanced church with effective evangelistic and social concern ministries: it was led by a dynamic pastoral team; it was light-years ahead of its time racially, incorporating persons from differing ethnic backgrounds into its life and leadership. This church experienced rapid growth, both numerically and spiritually.

Exercises: (1) Take a few minutes to write down three strengths of your church and three 'challenges'. Write constructively: 'challenges' are opportunities, not problems!
(2) Share your thoughts with your group, and write up a composite list, giving priority to the ideas expressed most frequently.

Further Reading: Kennon Callahan. *Twelve Keys to an Effective Church*, and *Effective Church Leadership: Building on the Twelve Keys*. San Francisco: Harper & Row, 1983, 1990; C. Peter Wagner. *Leading Your Church to Growth*. Ventura, Calif.: Regal Books, 1984; David Watson. *I Believe in the Church*. London: Hodder & Stoughton, 1978.

Photo: Northside Productions

1

The church as a critic of culture

(Chapters 1–10 may be studied with the help of video tape 2. The booklet accompanying the videos contains further discussion questions.)

I once talked with an Indian pastor who had been dragged many hundreds of metres through the streets of his town by militant Hindus, before being beaten with rods. 'What did you do?' I asked him. 'I blessed my persecutors in the name of the Lord' he said. 'And what happened?' 'The gospel fire was stoked up in my heart for these people!'

The church at Antioch was born out of persecution (Acts 11:19) as are churches in many parts of the world today. Persecution produces fewer half-Christians! Conversely, where there is little persecution and 'going to church' is a socially acceptable habit, nominalism becomes a deadly possibility. The greatest enemy of the church's health is not overt persecution, but affluence and apathy.

Culture is the sum total of a community's customs and values, which give it a sense of identity and continuity. No human culture is totally bad or totally good: we must challenge what is evil and affirm what is good in all cultures. As the evangelical Lausanne Covenant put it, culture must be tested and judged by scripture. Because humans are God's creatures, some of their cultures will be rich in beauty and goodness; because they are fallen, all of it is tainted with sin and some is demonic.

A 'cult of culture' develops when religion validates culture and society without bringing them under judgment. A certain social order becomes 'right' and therefore 'Christian' and cultural values are divinised. The prophetic dimension of our Hebraic-Christian tradition is lost. Love of neighbour becomes voluntary and is divorced from justice. Members of congregations are spared the pain of ethical examination of how structures and systems may be the instruments of injustice. The preacher is told to 'steer clear of politics' — and still be biblical and prophetic!

Such churches may claim they are 'neutral' and maintain the status quo; but there is no such thing as neutrality. Churches choosing to support what already exists may be supporting an ungodly system. Then, too, churches may contribute to the status quo by being preoccupied with their own internal affairs: administration, doctrine, buildings, finance, authority and liturgies.

When the church marries the spirit of this age, it will be widowed in the next. Jesus promised we would face trouble because his kingdom's values were in conflict with those of the world. 'Do not be conformed to the world', Paul warned (Romans 12:2). We are to be 'faithful in the alien', as Luke 16:12 reads literally. This earth and its cultures are not our final home. But we are not to abandon the earth. Rather we are to apply God's standards in it.

Discuss: (1) Where do our culture's values and beliefs differ from Jesus' understanding of the kingdom of God? (2) Stephen and his fellow-Christians were persecuted for confronting the powers-that-be by attacking their record of injustice. Would our church run any risk of persecution for this reason? (3) Apart from church-attending on Sundays, what distinguishes our church-members from people in the community who have no contact with the church? (4) If Jesus came back to our country, where would we find him, and what would he be doing — and saying?

Further Reading: Marvin K. Mayers. *Christianity Confronts Culture.* Grand Rapids: Zondervan, 1974; Charles Kraft. *Christianity in Culture.* Maryknoll: Orbis Books, 1979; Richard H. Niebuhr. *Christ and Culture.* New York: Harper & Row, 1956; Leonard Griffith. *Illusions of our Culture.* London: Hodder and Stoughton, 1969.

2

Towards an evangelistic lifestyle

The founders of this church wandered around 'speaking the word' (Acts 11:19–20, RSV), 'telling the message' (GNB). We don't know their names; they were probably not 'apostles' but ordinary Christians committed to sharing the good news with those they met. Churches everywhere are healthy or unhealthy to the extent that their members are verbalising their faith. Where this is left to 'professional' clergy or evangelists, those churches are diseased.

Evangelism is 'one beggar telling another beggar where to get food' (D. T. Niles). Jesus came to seek and to save the lost (Luke 19:10). The Lord is patient, because he does not want anyone to be destroyed, but wants all to turn away from their sins (2 Peter 3:9). It is God's desire that all hear the good news in such a way that they will turn from idols, i.e. living for anything other than God (1 Thessalonians 1:9). In the terms the New Testament uses, people either 'perish' or are 'saved' according to their response to this good news. And we, his people, are commissioned to preach it. What an awesome responsibility!

Peter Wagner (in *Your Church Can Grow*) says 10% of all Christians have a special evangelistic gift, but only about one half of one per cent are actively using it. Why is that? The other 90% are also 'gifted': all the spiritual gifts are meant to lead persons to

Christ. But let us hesitate before we launch 'total mobilisation' efforts: these often induce unnecessary guilt.

The most overtly 'evangelistic' Christians are the fundamentalists, who have a more literal view of hell. As we move towards the 'universalist' end of the theological spectrum ('everyone will be saved'; 'if there is a hell God will empty it'), evangelism becomes almost non-existent. Three other theologies which hinder evangelism are 'hyper-Calvinism' (God saves who he wants to save and rejects the rest; there's nothing we can do about that); anti-proselytism ('even if they are only nominal members of my church, don't you preach to them'); and syncretism ('all religions are valid; Christianity doesn't have all the answers'). What is your view?

Good evangelism is more than apologetics, which attempts to give a reasoned defense of the Christian faith. Apologetics cuts down trees; evangelism builds houses! Evangelism is more than imparting organised doctrine. As John Stott puts it, you have to win a person's confidence before you can win their soul! Do what Jesus did: minister to a 'felt need' first — for example, loneliness and poor self-image, sickness, hunger. John Stott told a conference on evangelism in Britain: 'Christians are more like the pharisees than Jesus. We keep our distance from people. We do not want to get hurt or dirty or contaminated'.

But good evangelism is more than being friendly: I come across 'friendly' churches that can't name many people who have committed their lives to Christ in the recent past. (Reason: new people change the chemistry of the group and we unconsciously freeze them out of our social life.) Good evangelism is more than inviting your neighbour to missions at the church. (Although these are valuable: your church ought to have regular special evangelistic efforts, appropriate to the culture of the people you are aiming to reach.) Evangelism is relating as Jesus did to people day by day, week by week. The best evangelism is done by new converts: they still have the most non-Christian friends! And the best evangelistic churches are where people truly love one another, especially across racial, social, cultural and other barriers which previously divided them.

Size per se is not an infallible measure of spiritual health. Some small churches are healthy, others malnourished; some large churches are healthy, others fat! However we can say that all healthy churches are experiencing additions by conversion, i.e. they grow!

Some of these growing churches give themselves away by adopting a 'mission mode', sending their trained members away to plant other churches, and so may not, over time, experience net numerical growth. That's alright. But I would be worried if my church were not causing the angels to have a party from time to time as people come into Christ's kingdom! The church at Antioch experienced rapid growth, both numerically and spiritually — though not all churches grow both ways at the same time! The acid test: list all the young people and adults who have come to Christ, joined the church and are growing in their faith in the last, say, ten years. Write down their names. In the 'great commission' (Matthew 28:19–20), there are four 'action verbs': going, making disciples, baptising and teaching. But only one ('make disciples') is in the imperative mood, the main command. Our central purpose is not merely to win converts, but to make disciples!

In the end, an evangelistic lifestyle arises out of the reality of our experience of Christ. If he has really changed our lives, that's great news and we'll want to share it!

Questions: (1) Discuss this statement from theologian Emil Brunner: 'The greatest sin of the church is that she withholds the gospel from herself and from the world'. (2) If you were to plan a strategy to acquaint everyone in your area about the facts of the good news, how would you do it? Why not do it? (3) In your group, tell one another how you would help a person who said to you, 'I want to become a Christian'.

Idea: Run a 'Christianity Explained' group for church members, new Christians and their non-Christian friends.

Further Reading: Peter Wagner. *Your Church Can Grow.* Glendale: Regal, 1976; David Watson. *I Believe in Evangelism.* London: Hodder and Stoughton, 1976.

3

Mature churches take risks

A l'il old lady protested to the vicar after a new prayer book was launched: 'If God were alive today, he'd be shocked at the changes in our church!'

In Antioch these evangelists 'jumped the culture barrier' and for the first time reached out to Gentiles. They were prepared to do something that had not been done before! When a church is hogtied to precedent ('we've not done it that way before') prepare for that church's funeral!

Cotton farmers in southern Alabama suffered two years' devastating losses thanks to the boll weevil. Some then tried a radically new idea, something they hadn't done before: they planted peanuts. It worked, they prospered and later erected a monument to the boll weevil!

Now tradition is important: it links us with our past and provides guidelines for the present. Community, church and family traditions build group cohesion and security. Sociologists tell us family routines such as 'grace' before meals, bedtime prayers with children, Christmas and birthday celebrations provide the 'glue' linking happy, memorable events together. Churches similarly have liturgical cycles and 'high days', as they celebrate what God has done in their history. 'Remember when ... ?' gives life meaning. Don't let hippies (who only have a 'present') or idealists (who only have a future) deprive you of your past!

But don't be a pain-in-the-neck nostalgic either. (They get a pain in the neck from constantly looking backwards.) For a mature individual or group, tradition is servant, not master. The present is not altogether to be interpreted by what has gone before. We must not be in bondage to a 'this-is-the-only-way-we-do-it-around-here' kind of immaturity. George Bernard Shaw used to talk about people who were 'dead at thirty and buried at sixty'! For a mature person there is security in risk-taking. In a life without risks no one wins, no one loses, and no one learns. Remember the lobster, which at a certain point in its life discards its outer protective shell and then becomes vulnerable to its enemies. Later it will grow a new 'house'. So become vulnerable! Encourage the young to see visions and the old to dream dreams.

Greek philosophers asked one another what element in life we could be most certain of and they answered 'change'. The only constant thing is change and, for a follower of the dynamic Christ, all of life must be seen as a process of growth. To be absolutely conservative is to deny the possibility of growth and reality being a moving, flowing process.

Probably 10%–20% of your people will never change; at the other end are 'early adopters' — also 10%–20%. The 'reluctant majority' will go along with change when they see its benefits outweigh the cost. There are three stages in the change process: resistance, tolerance, then approval. People must be given reasons for change: they must understand these reasons and see value in them.

Change is always experienced as loss, but it's not change that's the big problem for most people — it's change they can't control or that comes too quickly ('future shock'). This is why a good change agent will be consultative, allowing people to own the changes, exposing them to successful working models by visiting other churches, attending seminars, reading papers or books and will encourage experimental periods to test new ideas. Such a leader will both 'rule with a strong arm', but also 'gently lead' others (see Isaiah 40:10, 11).

Don't be in too great a hurry: make haste slowly. Sure, the Father created lots of things with a word; but the Son became one of us and lived among us, which took much longer! And all change must be bathed in prayer.

In an American basketball stadium hangs a large banner: 'IT CAN HAPPEN HERE!' It can happen in your life, in your church!

Discuss: (1) Analyse two innovations in your church — one that went wrong and another that succeeded. Why and why?

(2) Anticipate a future innovation (e.g. moving from one to two morning worship services). What would be a suitable countdown to ensure its successful adoption?

Further Reading: Lyle Schaller. *The Change Agent.* Nashville: Abingdon, 1970; Gerard Egan. *Change Agent Skills in Helping and Human Service Settings.* Monterey, California: Brooks/Cole, 1982; Denis Waitley. *Seeds of Greatness: The Ten Best-Kept Secrets of Total Success.* New Jersey: Revell, 1983.

4

Be evangelical or perish!

These missionaries announced the 'good news about the Lord Jesus' at Antioch (Acts 11:20). The gospel is more than a code of morals or ideas about civic duty; it is more than 'good views about the Lord Jesus,' says Stanley Jones. It is the good news that God loved us so much that he has taken the initiative to come to us (John 3:16), live among us as one of us (1 John 1:1), inviting us to turn from our sins and be reconciled to him (2 Corinthians 5:20). He even died for us (Romans 5:6-8), now offering us 'life in all its fullness' (John 10:10) as we are obedient to him as Lord in the church and in the world (John 14:21).

This is the historic gospel which the early Christian leaders urge their followers to 'guard' carefully (2 Timothy 1:14). Although this good news might have a different appeal to each person, churches committed to a sense of urgency (2 Timothy 4:2, JPB) about persuading people to receive Christ (John 1:12) are the only ones growing throughout the world.

A few years ago I wrote a little book called *Recent Trends Among Evangelicals* in which I pointed out the dangers of too narrow a definition of 'evangelicalism'. The word comes from the Greek *euangelion*, meaning good news. Some narrow the 'gospel' to an other-worldly 'pie in the sky when you die by and by', opting out of our social responsibility — a strong feature of the Judeo-Christian faith. Justice and love were, for Jesus, the two greatest 'kingdom values' (Matthew 22:36 ff; 23:23; Luke 11:42). And yet I can find no creed, confession of faith or evangelical doctrinal statement before about the 1960s (aside from the writings of John Wesley) — and very few recent ones — that mention explicitly either love or justice! It is very easy for evangelicals to be Pharisees!

The Christian faith is much more than believing propositions in your head and condemning others as heretics who do not dot your i's and cross your t's. In our gospel teaching, we need both heat and light — fervour and knowledge. Never forget that the Lord has yet more light and truth to break forth from his holy Word!

Discuss: (1) Try putting into about fifty words the essence of the Christian 'good news'. (Use passages like Matthew 23:23, Luke 11:42, 1 Corinthians 15:3-5, Acts 10:34-43 to help.) Share your summary with the group, and discuss variations in each person's attempt. Remember, however, the gospel is 'many-coloured': each New Testament writer gives a slightly different perspective on it, so our understandings will have a rich variety about them too. (2) If you had to put together a 'minimal creed' — the very basic affirmations all Christians should agree on — what would it say?

Further Reading: Rowland Croucher. *Recent Trends Among Evangelicals.* Sydney: Albatross, 1986 ($10 posted from John Mark Ministries, 7 Bangor Court, Heathmont, Australia 3135).

5

Communicate!

Communication (Latin *communis*, common) is creating 'commonness' with someone by sharing information, ideas, attitudes or feelings.

These preachers introduced their Gentile hearers in Antioch to Jesus as 'Lord' (Acts 11:20) not 'Christ' — a Jewish concept. (However, the fact that they allowed themselves later to be called 'Christians' by outsiders probably indicates that there were many Jewish believers in the group as well). These Gentiles knew all about 'lordship' — the Caesar to whom they paid their taxes was 'lord'. Earlier, Peter quoted Hebrew prophets to a Jewish audience (Acts 2:16ff.); later Paul quoted Greek poets to Athenians (Acts 17:22ff.).

So let us communicate to people 'on their turf', within their frame of reference (or 'field of experience'). Begin, as Jesus did, with people's life-situations 'scratching where people itch'. Jesus also taught (and prayed) in everyday language: a good reason for using Bible translations close to the language we speak (e.g. the *Good News Bible*). When young people tell us 'church is old-fashioned', we should listen carefully: some of us 'oldies' are very selfish when it comes to reaching a different generation. Quite frankly, if you ask 'persons in the street' what they think of the church, you might be surprised. Why don't you try it?. We need different 'packagings' for the unchanging product we bring, the gospel of the Lord Jesus.

About twenty years ago Gavin Reid wrote *The Gagging of God*, in which he said that the greatest threat to the gospel was not communism, apathy, humanism, impurity of doctrine or worldly compromise; rather, it was the breakdown of communication.' Western Christians tend to be message-centred ('we preach the message and God does the rest'), rather than audience-centred. The church utters billions of words and few are listening. We must be both message- and audience-centred. The receivers of our message see and hear what they want to see and hear: simply sending out messages will not guarantee a response. Unwanted communication is filtered out through selective attention, and the message may be understood differently to the meaning in the mind of the sender. So: give the message you want, but it's got to be packaged the way they want!

Within the church, let us create an 'open society', allowing folk to know what happens at leaders' meetings. The only exceptions would be sensitive issues of church discipline, or some negotiations for pastoral calls or property purchases. Have a 'church family time' during the worship services, as well as newsletters or bulletin boards. Informed church members are happier and better workers. The price of justice is eternal publicity!

Every secure pastor or church leader will invite feedback by formal and informal channels — for example, surveys, weekly 'care-cards', meeting people in groups. And when change agents want to steer people in a new direction they will utilise redundant communications — using two or more media, not just one! Simply because you've 'said' something doesn't mean communication has taken place.

But, of course, Christian communication is more than technique. What we are and what we do can cancel out or reinforce what we say ('the medium is the message'). And we grow spiritually and emotionally through expressing what makes up our inner experience. 'Behold how these Christians love one another' is the most powerful message of all to people outside the church (John 13:34-5). Such love communication will be genuine and compassionate, a deep 'commonness' of heart and mind. (Courses on 'listening skills' are good — but a loving person does it anyway!)

So communication is more than words. If your church sign says 'The end of your search for a friendly church' but you aren't greeted in a caring way or invited to anyone's home for lunch for a month, that communicates something! If the preacher is mostly 'against' lots of things, that communicates something! If people dress in a formal manner, wear sombre expressions and carry big black Bibles, that communicates something! If your buildings and grounds are not as neat as the average home in the neighbourhood, that communicates something, too. If you leave stale advertising around, that communicates sloppiness.

To sum up: Christian communication involves *kerygma* (good news), *martyria* (authentic witness), *diakonia* (loving service), *koinonia* (strengthening community), and *charisma* (spiritual power). Only life begets life, and a church that's alive communicates vibrancy and love in a very appealing way. When our message is clear, credible and compelling, people will respond to it — and to Christ.

Discuss: Seen on the notice-board of a small Christian sect: 'Services next Lord's Day (D.V.) — 11 a.m. and 7 p.m. No collection'. Text in the sanctuary of a middle-class Baptist church: 'I will not offer unto the Lord that which costeth me nothing'. What do these communicate?

Further Reading: Michael Green. *Evangelism in the Early Church.* London: Hodder & Stoughton, 1970,1978; Os Guinness. *The Dust of Death.* Downers Grove, Illinois: IVP, 1973; James F. Engel and H. Wilbert Norton. *What's Gone Wrong With the Harvest: A Communication Strategy for the Church and World Evangelism.* Grand Rapids: Zondervan, 1975.

6

Your cleverness isn't enough, however

If a church is evangelistic, has its doctrine right, is prepared to innovate and communicate effectively — surely that's a fairly complete list of qualities? Wrong.

Luke hastens to add that it's not the preacher's cleverness, the church's orthodoxy or its evangelistic strategies alone which lead people to new life in Christ, but the power (literally 'the hand') of the Lord (Acts 11:21). Certainly we need well-educated preachers, theologically and academically — modern-day equivalents to Moses, Daniel, Paul. But when the Lord's power invades a fisherman like Simon Peter, a shoe salesman like D. L. Moody, or a young American who's only done a couple of years in Bible colleges like Billy Graham, they can be very effective evangelists indeed. 'Correct' doctrine, homiletically-sound sermons, professional techniques all have their place, but throughout the world it is those churches that are open to the Lord's power working among them that are alive. Churches that have shunned this dimension in preference for a rationalistic faith are declining everywhere.

Introducing his *Letters to Young Churches*, J. B. Phillips stated:

> The great difference between present-day Christianity and that in these letters is that, to us, it is primarily a performance; to them it was a real experience. We reduce the Christian

religion to a code ... a rule of heart and life. To these it was quite plainly the invasion of their lives by a new quality of life altogether.

Perhaps you and your church are discouraged: in the face of the world's great needs what can you do? Peter, James, John and the others had a pretty straightforward task: preach the good news to the whole world! How were they to do it? 'When the Holy Spirit comes upon you, you will be filled with power' (Acts 1:8). 'Many of us,' wrote Charles G. Finney, 'want the peace Christ offers without the power he has also promised'. 'Come to the Son of Man', exhorts F. B. Meyer, 'so that he may supply that missing link, breathe power into you, baptise you in his sacred fire ...' Andrew Murray wrote: 'Take time. Give God time to reveal himself to you ... waiting to receive through the Spirit his power'.

'It is divine power we want, not better methods', said Hudson Taylor. 'Let us give ourselves to prayer for nothing less than to be filled with the Spirit, and made channels through which he shall work with resistless power.'

The nineteenth-century preacher C. H. Spurgeon thundered: 'It is extraordinary grace, not talent, that wins the day. It is extraordinary spiritual power, not extraordinary mental power, that we need ... Mental power may gather a congregation; spiritual power will save souls'.

Sometimes the great evangelists had a dynamic experience of the Holy Spirit. Let D. L. Moody tell his story:

One day in New York — oh what a day! — I cannot describe it. I seldom refer to it; it is almost too sacred an experience to name. Paul had an experience of which he never spoke for fourteen years. I can only say that God revealed himself to me, and I had such an experience of his love that I asked him to stay his hand. I went preaching again. The sermons were not different; I did not present any new truths; and yet hundreds were converted.

This same promise is also for us, who are 'afar off' (Acts 2:39).

But now a little note of caution. Recently I had lunch with a leader of Australia's fastest-growing denomination, the Assemblies of God. AOG pastors are poorly trained theologically compared with 'mainline' clergy. They are often on their own, battling away in lonely circumstances without much guidance from senior colleagues. But the Lord's power is with many of them and their churches are seeing more people converted to Christ than any other denomination in our country.

On the other hand, in the last three years I have spoken at half a dozen Anglican clergy conferences. The sophistication of these men (yes, men, but that will change before the second edition of this book!) theologically and liturgically was invigorating for this Baptist, but many of them minister year in and year out without seeing people grow significantly in faith.

Now most AOG pastors can't live with a plateauing or declining congregation: they feel they've failed if their church isn't growing numerically. Hasn't Yonggi Cho said the principles he uses to grow the largest church in the world in Korea are universal — they will work anywhere? On the other hand, Anglican sacramentalism and their concept of 'the cure of souls' enable many of them to do a 'maintenance' ministry for life and not be bothered by growth or the lack of it. My texts for each group come just four verses apart in Zechariah. Anglicans: 'You will succeed, not by might or by your own strength, but by my spirit says the Lord' (4:6). Pentecostals: 'Don't despise the day of small things' (4:10). My AOG friends should remember that it's God who 'gives the increase': their task is to be faithful and lead a church into spiritual maturity and health. And my Anglican friends ought to capture again the urgency of reaching the 'lost' with the good news, without necessarily surrendering their great traditions.

Growing churches can become conceited, despising others for their lack of evangelistic effectiveness. There is pride of place, pride of race, pride in the gifts of nature and even pride in the gifts of the Spirit. But then the mainline churches despise the lack of sophistication among fundamentalists or pentecostals. We all live in a status jungle, sharing a need for significance with baboons, jackdaws, roosters and swordtail fish! Academic theologians despise the uneducated, and fiery pentecostal preachers despise the 'religiosity' of theologians who are 'dying by degrees'. Pride, said C.S. Lewis, gets no pleasure out of having something, only out of having more of it than the next person. All snobbery is irreligious and unintelligent (James 2:1-13). Mary in her *Magnificat* declared that the Lord will scatter the proud, bringing down the mighty from their thrones.

In the early church, word and Spirit went hand in hand. In Western Christianity, we have tended to be more word than Spirit, with the exception of the Pentecostals/Charismatics, who may sometimes have an imbalance the other way. Our theology has been very cerebral, with little openness to the power of the Holy Spirit. Throughout the world, where 'signs and wonders' accompany the proclamation of the good news, the church is dynamic and alive. However the great need for those young churches is Bible teaching — but without losing their enthusiasm. More of that later.

Discuss: Write for the *GRID* article mentioned below, and talk about the twenty issues there.

Further Reading: David Watson. *One in the Spirit.* London: Hodder and Stoughton, 1973; and *I Believe in the Church.* London: Hodder and Stoughton, 1978; C. Peter Wagner. *How to Have a Healing Ministry Without Making Your Church Sick.* Ventura: Regal Books, 1988; and *The Third Wave of the Holy Spirit.* Ann Arbor: Servant Publications, 1988; John Wimber and Kevin Springer (eds). *Riding the Third Wave: What Comes After Renewal?* Scoresby, Vic.: Canterbury Press, 1988; Rowland Croucher. 'Charismatic Renewal: Myths and Realities', *GRID*, World Vision of Australia (Box 399C Melbourne, Australia 3001).

7

The disease of nominalism

A mother tucked her little girl into bed, prayed with her, and went downstairs. Soon she heard a loud 'thump'. Running upstairs, she found her daughter on the floor. 'What happened?' she asked. 'P'raps, Mummy, I went to sleep too near where I got in!'

Many congregations are like that. Ask 'How is your faith growing?' and they can't answer. They follow the ABC of church adherence — attend, believe, contribute — but are still spiritual pygmies.

These new converts at Antioch believed. They put their faith in the Lord. This is an important idea. Let's look at it more closely.

What is faith?

There are two kinds of faith: *fides*, faith or belief that, and *fiducia*, faith in. Both kinds of faith are gifts from God, available to everyone (Ephesians 6:23, 2:8, 9). Belief about God is necessary before we can have faith in him. So God graciously reveals himself to us in nature, history, the prophets, the community of faith, and supremely in Jesus. When we read the Bible or hear the preacher and become convinced in our minds that this God is worth entrusting one's life to, we make the big commitment and become a Christian: this time with our hearts, our wills, our whole life. Then we begin to nurture and exercise our faith to make it grow. The apostles asked Jesus to increase their faith (Luke 17:5). Jesus said, 'Everything is possible to the one who has faith' (Mark 9:23).

So, in essence, faith means trust; as the Sunday school anagram has it 'Forsaking all I trust him'. It's the essence of a relationship with someone — in this case, the Lord. Without faith it is impossible to please God (Hebrews 11:6). It's not 'faith in faith'; it's not a 'leap into the dark'; it's not 'believing what you cannot prove'. It's faith in a faithful God.

What you need to begin the Christian life is not great faith in God but faith in a great God! You don't have to have all the answers — just as you don't have to know all about electricity before you switch on the light. Jesus asked a man with a withered arm to stretch it forth — the one thing he couldn't do. But with the little faith he had, he tried — and the arm became well. Use the little faith you've got, not someone else's faith you haven't got.

Faith is trusting the Lord, even when we sometimes don't understand his ways. But faith doesn't mean switching off your reason. In 18th century Europe many churches had to make a fearful decision: should they install lightning rods? Some said no, and attempted to appease the Almighty by ringing the church bells during thunderstorms (and 12 German bell-ringers died in a 33 year period). The congregation of the church of San Nazaro in Brescia, Italy, not only rejected the protection of lightning rods but also had sufficient faith in the sanctity of their church to store 100 tons of gunpowder in its vaults. In 1767, lightning struck the church and ignited the gunpowder, causing an explosion which destroyed one-sixth of the city and killed 3000 people. (Snake-handlers in rural America have died for similar silliness!) Jeremiah told the Jews not to believe they were safe simply because 'this is the Lord's Temple, this is the Lord's Temple, this is the Lord's Temple' (Jeremiah 7:1–4).

But as our faith grows, and we know the God in whom we trust is loving and utterly faithful, we sometimes have to trust him when our 'reason' can't supply all the answers. Have you heard of the man who was mountain climbing in the American Rockies along a very rugged track? Suddenly he slipped, falling over a cliff. He grabbed the roots of a tree and hung there. When he got his breath back, he looked down and saw an enormous drop. If he fell, he'd certainly be killed. Looking up, the cliff top was so far above him he couldn't climb back. In desperation, although he knew he was alone, he cried out 'Is anyone up there?' He was startled to hear a booming voice say 'Yes!' 'Can you help me?' 'Yes' came the response. 'What must I do?' The voice answered, 'Let go!'. There was a long pause, then finally the man called out, 'Is anybody else up there?'

How does faith grow?

A step at a time. In my files, there are about two hundred stories of people who've had a strong faith. They all had these features in common:

(1) Their faith grew because they had a particular view of God — a God who is always available, who loves us, who desires the best for us. So their faith is in a God who believes in us, as well as our believing in him! This God is powerful, and is the same as he ever was.

So (2) they fed their faith on the stories in the Bible, reading them over and over again: if God did it for them, he'll do it for me!

(3) They noted the importance of faith in the teachings of Jesus (Matthew 8:10/Luke 7:9; Matthew 9:2/Mark 2:5/Luke 5:20; Matthew 9:29; Matthew 15:28; Mark 11:22; Luke 7:50; Luke 8:25/Mark 4:35–41/Matthew 8:23–27).

(4) They used the faith they had, not the faith they didn't have. And they were obedient in their use of that faith. In Luke 17, Jesus says we should forgive someone who sins against us seven times in one day! The disciples ask — reasonably enough we might think — for more faith to do this. Jesus brushes off the request, saying, in effect, 'What you need isn't more faith, but using the faith you already have! Your problem isn't faith or the lack of it, but obedience!' To grow stronger, you don't need a muscle transplant, but to exercise the muscles you have! Trust and obey says the old hymn — and it's still true.

(5) They think of possibilities. Just as Augustine wrote the biography of sin in four words -: a thought, a form, a fascination, a fall — so faith begins with your thoughts of faith. So they 'image' possibilities, believing 'all things are possible to the one who believes'. They link their faith to a vision.

(6) They verbalise this commitment to a dream — they talk to themselves! They repeat faith-formulas in their prayer and to themselves: 'I can do all things through Christ who strengthens me' (Philippians 4:13). 'Perfect love casts out fear' (1 John 4:18).

(7) But they aren't off-the-planet idealists: they analyse situations; they research the whole thing; they get all the facts together; they find a need and fill it; they become consumed with this vision; they organise and plan to reach their God-inspired destiny.

(8) Once they've used their minds in all these ways, they are

prepared to take risks. The story of Abraham leaving his secure home and country to ride off into the west appeals to them greatly!

(9) They follow Paul's advice in Philippians 4:8: 'Whatever is true, noble, right, pure, lovely and honourable ... keep on thinking about these things'. Just as a clean engine gives more power, so a clean life is more in tune with the infinitely powerful God.

(10) They feed their faith by discipline and hard work.

Making faith real

There are many in our churches who believe God exists, but haven't really surrendered their lives to God. For them 'the faith' is a body of beliefs they affirm in the creed — 'faith about' God but not yet faith in God. The church is thus a social club with a religious flavour. It is very dangerous when such a church elects uncommitted people to high office. A church that's alive will be stretching their people's faith all the time.

How do they do that? Here are some clues: (1) How often are people other than the pastor/vicar encouraged to verbalise their commitment to Christ (in preaching, teaching adults, leading worship etc.)? (2) Does the preaching issue a clear call for commitment? (3) What happens to new converts to encourage them to grow spiritually? (4) How many of the Sunday attenders are in small Bible study groups? If it's less than 50%, I'd be worried. (5) Similarly, what proportion of committee members, etc.? If it's less than 80%, you've got a problem. (6) What opportunities (other than Sunday school teaching) are offered for direct verbal evangelism? (7) How many have been motivated enough to enter Bible or theological college? (8) How many home-grown, full-time missionaries has your church sent out? Can you think of some other faith indicators?

Discuss: # How can a congregation avoid the disease of nominalism? How does your church measure up? # Study the 'Empowerment questionnaire' in the Appendix. How does your church rate?

8

Penitence and holiness

A great number at Antioch 'turned to the Lord' (Acts 11:21). This is 'repentance', responding to the warning 'Turn around — you are going the wrong way!' Repentance is the opposite of blaming; it is 'owning' my sinfulness rather than off-loading the blame somewhere else.

Sigmund Freud, more than any other modern psychologist, has changed our understanding of ourselves at this point. He has located many of our personality disorders in the early experiences of infancy. These, he said, were repressed into our subconscious and come back later to haunt us.

Now this may be true, but it may also distort our perspective and cause us to have a 'blame-oriented' approach to life. Scientific sanction is given to a tendency as old as our history — attacking the problem of evil by laying the blame on someone else. The biblical prophets tried to steer us away from externalising our problems and saying 'out there' to internalising them and admitting 'in here'. Jesus' first public words were about repentance, as were his last, when he commissioned his followers to take his message of salvation to all peoples: 'There is forgiveness of sins for all who turn to me' (Luke 24:47).

Repentance involves a change of mind (conviction); Jesus illustrated this in the story of the two sons (Matthew 21:28, 29). We must also be sorry for our sins (contrition; Psalm 38:18). Then, there is confession: in Jesus' famous story the prodigal went to his father and said, 'I have sinned both against heaven and you' (Luke 15:18, 21). A fourth element in true repentance is forsaking our sins (Isaiah 55:7), — 'owning then disowning' them. To refuse to repent is worse than the sin for which one ought to repent. Or, in the grim words of Samuel Davies, 'The question is not, shall I repent? For that is beyond a doubt. The question is, shall I repent now when it may save me; or shall I put it off to the eternal world when my repentance shall be my punishment?'

'Believing' plus 'repentance' equals conversion. Although we begin the Christian way through a conversion, there will certainly be many 'conversions' along the Christian way as well. These transitions or 'movements' happen when we are renewed, turned around, see things differently (with God's gift of insight). As Henri Nouwen says in his book *Reaching Out*, there will be movements from loneliness to solitude, hostility to hospitality, illusion to prayer. The essence of all conversion, however, is the movement from sinfulness to forgiveness, from alienation to belonging: and then from territoriality (my space — keep out) to hospitality (my space — you're welcome).

Converted people are holy people. They are saved, yes, but they want to be 'more saved'! Billy Graham, who has probably spoken to more people face-to-face than anyone else, is still preaching the gospel fifty years after his first sermon. He does not keep any of his speaking fees or royalties from his books. From the very beginning of his career, says the evangelist, 'I was frightened — I still am — that I would do something to dishonour the Lord'.

That's holiness! If your church's brand of Christianity is turning out truly converted — changed — people, it's a live church!

Discuss: W. E. Sangster, in his booklet 'How Much Are You Saved?' says the Bible sometimes talks about conversion as 'being saved' (Acts 2:47). One of his tests: 'You are "saved" if your concern for a world of needy persons translates into action'. Is it possible to be saved and selfish? 'God loved the world' — how much do we love the world (of people)?

9

Interdependence — a sign of maturity

The young, dynamic group of believers at Antioch came to the attention of the believers in the mother church at Jerusalem. They sent Barnabas to help establish the church who, with Saul of Tarsus, worked hard to help these young Christians grow in their faith.

Dependence is the essence of childhood, independence of adolescence, interdependence of mature adulthood. Many of our churches are not yet adult. They are territorial, hence the notion of 'sheep-stealing'. Most churches don't know what the church of their own denomination in the next suburb is doing. I believe the Lord of the church wants all the shepherds in an area to express their unity by working, praying and planning together: they should regard each other as fellow-workers, not competitors for each others' sheep!

The church at Jerusalem felt a oneness with the young church at Antioch. As you read the New Testament letters, this sort of 'bonding' is quite normal.

Jesus had a unifying vision for his church and prayed that she 'may become perfectly one' (John 17:20–23). C. H. Spurgeon once said: 'This prayer was not only the casual expression of the

Saviour's desire at the last, but is the sort of model of the prayer which is incessantly going up from him to the eternal throne'. The Holy Spirit has been given to the church to form the body of Christ, knit together into one body those different persons who believe in Jesus. If another has something against us, we ought to attempt reconciliation before we worship (Matthew 5:23–24). Peter had to learn that what God had cleansed had to be acceptable to him also. Later, defending his acceptance of Cornelius to the other apostles he says 'If God gave the same gift to them as he gave to us when we believed in the Lord Jesus Christ, who was I that I could withstand God?' (Acts 10:9 to 11:18). In Ephesians, we are told that there is a spiritual unity between believers anyway; and the good news breaks down the walls that divide us. One of the most serious sins in the early churches was schism (1 Corinthians 11:18).

So we do not manufacture Christian unity; we maintain it. One of the hallmarks of a 'sect' or 'cult' is that it defines who are saved or lost very narrowly — the saved are pretty much confined to their own group.

A home and family can be a unity despite differences of temperament — because we are children of the same parents. So the thing that binds the family of God together is not that we agree on everything, but the fact that we are all children of the same Father. Immaturity in a church is manifest when we expect others to believe the same as we do before we'll have full fellowship with them. We wait until we can all sing in unison, where we should be singing in harmony! Disunity in the name of Christ is a scandal and a shame, but it is nothing new — even Jesus had to deal with it. One day Jesus' friends found someone casting out demons in his name and told him to stop, on the ground that 'he doesn't belong to our group'. But Jesus rebuked them: 'Do not try to stop him, because whoever is not against you is for you (Luke 9:49–50).

Why is there still disunity? (1) First there may be a fear that we will lose our 'distinctiveness'. But what we have in common with others is more important than what divides us. What God has taught others (their distinctiveness) ought to be added to ours. (2) Denominational pride: we ought to be thankful for all the Lord has given and taught our group; but let us be humbly thankful for what we can learn from others. (3) This one is more sinister: disunity is a demonic tactic and many Christian churches and sects have fallen for it! So it's a spiritual battle we're waging here (Ephesians 6:12). Satan has a direct interest in keeping the body of Christ divided and weak — encouraging Christians to forget who their real enemy is so they'll be in conflict with one another. Satan knows and fears a united church; he knows the gates of hell will not prevail against Christ's church, but he also knows a house divided against itself cannot stand.

According to Romans 15:7, we are to receive and accept one another not on the basis of having the same creeds or clichés, but on the basis of Christ's acceptance of us. Whoever demands more than faith in Christ in order to be accepted by God makes the death of Christ unnecessary (Galatians 2:21). We ought to define persons not in terms of their being Presbyterian, Catholic, Pentecostal or whatever, but rather on the basis of their acknowledging Jesus Christ as Lord.

John Calvin wrote to Archbishop Thomas Cranmer, the man largely responsible for the Anglican Book of Common Prayer: 'The churches are so divided that human fellowship is scarcely now of any repute ... So much does this concern me that if I could be of any service, I would not begrudge traversing ten seas for this purpose.'

When we are united we become more mature, like our Lord Jesus Christ (Ephesians 4:13). Churches need each other. Let us love one another, help one another, work together to spread God's shalom throughout a very needy world.

Research: Contact the 8–10 nearest Christian churches, and draw up a list of items they would like you to pray about. Feed these into your church's prayer groups.

10

The best committees are committees of one!
(or, was that meeting really necessary?)

'Mr Chairman I move we colour the ladies' toilet lilac, make the mens' toilets orange.' In church-meeting folk-lore, issues such as this have divided congregations down the middle.

The British Weekly ran an article beginning: 'I spent an hour this morning with ten prisoners and, as we separated, I said to myself very firmly, 'Never again'. Our meeting was not behind barred walls ... but in a suburban vestry'. Peter Drucker, the management specialist, tells us the church can be run with one-tenth of the committees they have without the slightest impairment of anything.

When the 'authorities' in Jerusalem heard about some unusual happenings in far-off Antioch, they did what headquarters always do when people are creative: they sent a committee to investigate (Acts 11:22).

It was a committee of one person: Barnabas, a Jew from Cyprus, who may have been converted with many other 'foreign' Jews at Pentecost. He was held in high esteem by the Jerusalem apostles (and maybe by others as well, which is perhaps why he didn't flee the city after the persecution). He was a good choice. Barnabas was able to understand both the Jewish and Greek mindsets. Like Paul, he was brought up as a Jew, actually a Levite, but outside Palestine.

'Committees of one' are always the best committees in the church. Most effective ministry gets done by one person with vision, energy and commitment. Dr W. E. Sangster put it well in one of his Westminster sermons:

How were the slaves freed? Did all England wake up one morning and say, 'This is wrong. We must free the slaves'? No! One man woke up one morning with the groan of God in his soul and William Wilberforce and his friends laboured until Britain paid a larger sum than her national debt to set the slaves free.

How was all the social trouble after the industrial revolution ameliorated? God groaned in the heart of Lord Shaftesbury and he toiled and toiled to serve and save the poor. How were the prisons cleaned up in England? Did everybody suddenly say, 'These prisons are places of indescribable filth'? No! God groaned in the heart of Elizabeth Fry. Progress is the echo of the groan of God in the hearts of [individual] men and women.[1]

Committees of one get things done! However, in a responsible community, that person ought to be accountable to the leaders God has placed in the church, so a clear ministry description should be mutually agreed upon, with boundaries of authority clearly understood. In addition, such persons ought to be encouraged to consult and work with others where appropriate. We don't want the church to become a hive of activist 'loners' doing their own thing because they can't get along with other people.

Committees don't have a 'good press' in most churches. 'Groups of people who take minutes and waste hours.' 'Devices to keep people away from families and spiritual exercises.' 'What happened to the unicorns? They tried to get into the ark by committee.' 'In the first place God made idiots — this was for practice; then he made boards' (Mark Twain). So run the cynics' comments.

In a cartoon the chairman says to three or four bored people around a table: 'You've heard of art for art's sake? This is meeting for meeting's sake!'

More seriously: 'Committees of rational people can be expected to act less rationally than their members' (Kenneth Arrow).

Many pastors and leaders think that if you want to involve someone in the life of the church, invite him or her to join a committee and they'll feel wanted, active, part of the group. That's a fallacy. For one thing, many amateurs run church committees and run them very poorly, creating frustration in those who give high priority to spending time fruitfully. Further, the best happenings in life involve openness, warmth, trust and spontaneity — most of which may be missing when a group meets as functionaries rather than as brothers and sisters. 'Bureaucracy is a way of carrying out transactions among strangers.'

But there's a more subtle temptation: the Devil would prefer people to join committees rather than growth or cell groups where they may develop spiritually. No one should be a committee member, except as an occasional advisor, who does not already belong to a Bible study/prayer group. However, with all this said, church members need the satisfaction of knowing what's going on. They ought to be part of the decision-making processes of the church and they ought to feel their contributions of time and ideas are valued.

Anthropologists tell us that almost all the world's cultures have three things in common: sex, war and committees. So if your church is going to have committees of more than one, and that's inevitable, here's some wit and wisdom I once heard from Lyle Schaller, which could save your church's life:

What's legal? In Germany everything's prohibited unless permitted; in France everything's permitted unless prohibited; in the USSR everything's prohibited including most things permitted. With standing committees everything is prohibited unless permitted (continuity's the key word); with study committees everything is permitted unless prohibited; ad hoc/action committees do things rather than study them: they can't adjourn until their job is done. Middle-sized churches need more standing committees to take the load off the board. Small churches need more ad hoc committees, with authority to act. Large churches need more of all three. Why don't cows fly? Because that's not the nature of cows. Don't expect standing committees to create or implement ideas: they're cemeteries for ideas. Give half-baked ideas to a study committee to be tidied up. Action committees get things done (they should have 3, 5, or 7 people — an odd number). If a new program is envisaged, create a new committee to get it going if you want new people involved. If a large sum is given to the church, give it to non-trustees to decide its destiny (trustees vote for continuity rather than a new ministry: for 'trustees' read whoever are the 'permission-witholders' in your church — and every church has them!).[2]

In other words, committees are process-oriented, ideas-oriented or action-oriented. You'd better decide your committee's purpose before you launch it. Many crises in church structure are crises of objectives, not of organisation.

As a general rule, the larger the committee the more cumbersome it is. Committee people should have sufficient data before the meeting, to pray and make informed decisions. The meeting's purpose should be clear and announced early. Always have some sort of agenda and suggested time-frame. With literate groups, assume the minutes are read: they should be action-oriented, with a column for persons responsible for what to whom by when.

Ask the best chairperson to do that job: he/she will have integrity (i.e. not a manipulator), will be an amateur psychologist (people have all sorts of agendas other than those spoken), will move things along, firmly control 'talk machines' and 'suggestion squelchers', delegate work to people between meetings (or encourage not meeting at all if there are insufficient reasons) and lead the committee to 'own' their work (rather than be a rubber stamp of someone else's). Have some sort of evaluation of your meetings: say ten minutes at the end. You'll be surprised how open people are in assessing what's going on.

Jacques Ellul has a sober word to say about obligatory prayer at the opening of business meetings of the church:

> The intention is good ... (but they can in reality be) purely formal prayers to cover the mediocrity of our decisions. They are a kind of official prayer, which allows us afterward to manage according to our own ideas ... without giving God the slightest chance to express his will. Such prayers (can be) an affront to the honour of God.[3]

Let us take note!

A final word on committees: beware the 'mythology of achievement', i.e. the belief that once you've talked you have done something!

And the colour of the church restrooms? Never discuss things like that in a church meeting! Give the decision to three people whose homes have the best decor.

Discuss: (1) Do a diagnostic test on your church's committees: what should be done by one person? Are there committees for the right things? Are they the right size? Are people on committees in some sort of spiritual growth context? (2) How well do your people know what's going on? By what formal or informal channels do they find out? (3) Where are decisions really made in your church (e.g. wives of board members, over the farm fence, etc.)?

NOTES
1. W. E. Sangster, *Westminster Sermons* (London: The Epworth Press, 1960), p. 84.
2 Lyle Schaller (heard at a church leaders' conference in Dallas, 1986).
3 Jacques Ellul, *Prayer and Modern Man* (New York: Seabury, 1979), p. 19.

11

Barnabas the encourager: may his tribe increase

(Video tape 3 has more on the material in chapters 11–20.)

If one part of Christ's body is praised, all the other parts share its happiness (1 Corinthians 12:26). A church of encouragers is a church that's alive. Discouragement is a sure sign of disease in Christ's body. 'The deepest principle in human nature', said William James, 'is the craving to be appreciated'. 'Therefore encourage one another and build each other up' (1 Thessalonians 5:11).

Barnabas' name was Joseph, but was changed to 'son of encouragement'. He must have been the sort of person who left a trail of encouraged people behind him wherever he went. The various episodes in the New Testament where he appears from time to time bear this out. If your friends gave you a nickname, would you be likely to get one like 'Encourager'? When he arrived he certainly 'barnabised' them (Acts 11:23).

Gene Getz has a helpful book on the 'one another' passages of the New Testament. In the final chapter — 'Encourage One Another' — he points out that the Greek word *parakaleo* has several related meanings: to exhort, admonish, teach, beg, entreat, beseech, console, encourage, comfort: But the basic word is always used for one primary purpose — to describe functions that will help Christians to be built up in Christ, or to help them to build up one another in Christ ...

Evaluate your church structure in view of this New Testament exhortation. Many traditional churches are designed not for 'body function' but for 'preacher function'. Only the pastor or minister or some other teacher is delegated to share the Word of God with others in the church ... The Bible teaches that every Christian must be involved in this process (1 Thessalonians 5:11, Hebrews 10:24–25) ... One thing stands out as being very important in this ministry — the 'body of Christ'. Every member contributes to its success.[1]

Like Jesus, you must always be gentle with the wounded, and — only if you have earned the right — occasionally be tough with the lazy or those whose potential may be realised more by rebuke than a soft word. Helpful criticism should always, or nearly always, leave the person feeling he/she has been helped.

Goethe said: 'If you treat people as they are they will stay as they are. But if you treat them as they ought to be, they will become bigger and better persons'. There are more 'win-win' conflict resolutions around than we realise! Churches are often inept at encouraging their leaders.

John Claypool in a sermon said that what often happens in life (is that) a person is given a difficult job by a group of people and then, instead of struggling with him and helping him find his way, the group sits back and lets him struggle alone until at last he 'hangs himself'.

James Stewart quotes this legend: God decided to reduce the weapons in the devil's armoury to one. Satan could choose which 'fiery dart' he would keep. He chose the power of discouragement. 'If only I can persuade Christians to be thoroughly discouraged', he reasoned, 'they will make no further effort and I shall be enthroned in their lives'.

Let me share a personal story about encouragement. I came to the Blackburn Baptist Church in Victoria, Australia, when it had about 300 members. Within five years, the membership had risen to over 700 (with over 1000 attending) — the largest Baptist church in the country. How? Why? If I were to name one key factor it would be that the 'BBC' was a church of encouragers. No Sunday would ever pass in the last few years of my leadership there without my pockets bulging with affirming notes from people. Sometimes we'd incorporate an 'encouragement segment' into a service and write encouraging messages to others.

If we appreciated someone or their ministry, we'd give ourselves permission to tell them! People are healed by encouragement; they grow to like themselves in a healthy way if they're encouraged; they reduce their 'self despising' through encouragement. Beware of a church of encouragers: you're going to have space problems after a while! May Barnabas' tribe increase in our churches: God knows we desperately need more church members like him.

An eighty-year-old saint once wrote me a note:
If he earns your praise bestow it;
If you like him let him know it;
Let words of true encouragement be said.
Do not wait till life is over,
And he's underneath the clover;
For he cannot read his tombstone when he's dead!
Suspect theology, but wise psychology!

However, all that said, let me add a note of caution. My desk calendar today reads, 'People ask you for criticism, but they only want praise'. We can depend so much on positive feedback that such praise becomes addictive: we cannot function without it.

A young monk, one of the 'desert fathers', looked after his elder who was gravely ill for twelve years without interruption. Never once in that period did his elder thank him or so much as speak one word of kindness to him. Only on his deathbed did the old man remark to the assembled brethren, 'He is an angel and not a man'. The story illustrates the need for 'detachment' although it could be argued the old man took his side of things a bit far!

Bible Study: Using a concordance, Bible dictionary and commentaries, prepare a group Bible study on 'Barnabas: The Ministry of Encouragement'.

A Prayer:
Lord, give me a ministry:
   not of pulling down, but of building up.
Help me to encourage, to uphold and to understand.
   Give me a ministry:
not so much of confrontation, as of reconciliation.
   Not so much of criticism as of intercession.
That life might be a prayer and a benediction for those
   You love.[2]

NOTES

1 Gene Getz, *Building Up One Another* (Wheaton, Illinois: Victor Books, 1976), pp. 110–120.

2 Barbara N. Woods, *Decision* magazine, October 1982.

Photo: Eddy Marmur

12

The gift of sanctified permissiveness

Two people look up to a cloudy sky. One sees a threat of rain, the other a promise of rain.

When I was in South Africa, a black pastor told me his church had a written order for public prayer for healing but they never used it. Why? 'Because white hands may have to be laid on black heads!'

Fear, pride or ignorance are behind the slogan, 'We've not done it that way before!'

Although what happened in Antioch was outside Barnabas' experience, he was a big enough person to believe that God was doing a new thing. How often church leaders are bound by history, especially the history of their own group. God isn't allowed to step outside the structures and habits and orthodoxies of one's own church or denomination! Many of us are so threatened when God does something new we react according to the mindless adage, 'If you don't understand it, condemn it or discourage it!'

The history of the church is beset with a litany of blinkered leaders committing the sin of unbelief. Small minded people cannot believe that God is versatile enough to operate in ways beyond our experience and understanding. This is the kind of arrogant pride that has seen prophets killed, change resisted and renewal discouraged.

When the Spirit of God fell on seventy leaders (Numbers 11:25ff.) and they began to 'shout like prophets', Joshua couldn't cope and told Moses to stop them. Moses replied, 'I wish the Lord would give his Spirit to all his people and make all of them shout like prophets!' We can understand Joshua's fear of what is new and strange, but Moses had the larger view.

Today, as I type this, Psalm 78 is the lectionary psalm, where the Israelites are berated for sinning against God by believing his power was limited to their experience (Psalm 78:17–20).

When the Messiah came and his opponents said, 'Prophets do not come from Galilee' (John 7:52), they were expressing the same sort of blinkered unbelief.

When Savonarola in Florence, Jan Hus in Bohemia, the Englishmen Wycliffe and Tyndale, or Luther in Germany advocated reform in a decadent church, the powers-that-be persecuted them. When the Anabaptists preached doctrines commonly held today, thousands were burnt by Catholics or drowned by Protestants. Because Servetus had ideas John Calvin didn't agree with, he was executed by burning. When Wesley tried to 'reform the church and spread scriptural holiness over the land' churches closed their doors to him, so he went into the market places and countryside.

When William Carey suggested that God wanted the gospel preached to the far corners of the earth, he was told to 'Sit down. When God wants the heathen converted, he'll do it without your help or mine!' When the Plymouth Brethren opposed formalism and spiritual deadness in the nineteenth century British churches and advocated a return to apostolic simplicity, they were often criticised as untutored and ignorant. (But when Christian Brethren people today have an experience of the Holy Spirit that is too 'charismatic', they too are sometimes persecuted.)

When some brave German Christians opposed Hitler, Alfred Delp (a Jesuit), Dietrich Bonhoeffer (a Lutheran), and others were executed. Indeed, more Christians may have been persecuted, tortured and slain in this century than any other. In many places it is dangerous to be a Christian — particularly a Christian who helps the poor.

A pastor, in a church which believes baptism is essential for salvation, quoted one of their sayings: 'Now abideth faith, hope and love — and the greatest of these is baptism'! (For other groups, substitute 'bishops', 'tongues', 'sacraments', 'Saturday sabbath', 'ecumenism', '1662 prayer book', 'Latin Mass' or whatever.)

It must be interesting for the angels to look down on our planet to see thousands of different denominations, each one believing it has a monopoly on the truth, and that heaven is going to be populated only with people like them!

The body of Christ, Paul affirms, comprises people with different spiritual gifts, who serve the Lord in different ways, with different abilities, but who all affirm 'Jesus is Lord!' and in whose lives the Spirit's presence is shown (1 Corinthians 12:1–7).

Stanley Jones asked a missionary how they obtained such a lovely property, and was told: 'The man who owned it built such high and expensive walls he went bankrupt and had to sell the property'. Bankrupt — building walls! Is that not a parable of our churches?

Discuss: (1) If your church were to become divided over some issue of doctrine or method, what might that issue be? (2) What are your church's 'distinctives'? What can you learn from what God has taught other churches?

13

Get with it — be committed!

Every good sermon, say teachers-of-preachers, can be summarised (by both preacher and congregation) in one sentence. Barnabas preached to the new converts at Antioch and his message, as Luke summarises it: 'Be faithful and true to the Lord with all your hearts' (Acts 11:23). As Australians would say, 'Get fairdinkum!' Don't be a half-hearted Christian! Be committed!

Commitment involves change, growth, fervour, enthusiasm. 'Enthusiasm' comes from two Greek words — *en* (in) *theos* (God), so the word literally means 'one possessed by God (or the gods)'. Enthusiasm literally means being full of God. Christian enthusiasts are concerned above everything else with what God wants (Matthew 6:33). Being a Christian is the most exciting thing in all the world!

Charles Schwab, the American industrialist who rose from poverty to put the US Steel Corporation together, once said, 'You can succeed at almost anything for which you have unlimited enthusiasm'. Emerson said, 'Nothing great was ever achieved without enthusiasm'. And here's another quote from my desk calendar: 'Years wrinkle the skin, but lack of enthusiasm wrinkles the soul'. Which reminds me of Thoreau's 'None are so old as those who have outlived enthusiasm'. Most people get enthusiastic about something, as you will discover at a football match, in a disco, or at a political convention. However, as Billy Graham once said, 'It is very strange that the world accepts enthusiasm in every realm, but the spiritual'. Those who have achieved great things for God have been people of infectious zeal and unquenchable enthusiasm.

John the Baptist was one of these. Jesus said he was a bright and shining light, a light that blazed and shone. But John the Baptist had earlier said that Christ would baptise with the Holy Spirit and with fire. How do we get on fire for God?

The early Christians were people on fire for God. 'We can't help speaking', they said, 'of the things we have seen and heard'. Jeremiah was like that. He could not keep God's message to himself. It was like a fire burning deep within him. He'd tried to hold it back but could not (Jeremiah 20:9).

In growing churches, everywhere, the commitment-expectations are higher than in declining churches. The second largest Pentecostal congregation in Australia expects twenty (yes, twenty) hours of ministry each week from each member. And that church is booming!

Generally speaking, leaders get the level of commitment they expect. Quintilian laid it down as a first principle of rhetoric that the orator who wishes to set the people on fire must himself be burning. Because church people are in a sense a pastor's employers, there's a temptation for the pastor to soften the prophetic side of ministry, opting to pitch the commitment level within the 'comfort zone' of the people. Where ecclesiastical wineskins are bereft of new wine, the church becomes stale, lifeless. There may be order, but as British Anglican David Watson used to say often, it's the orderliness of the cemetery.

Now there's another side to all this. 'Dead churches are afraid of enthusiasm'; that's true, but enthusiasm has a history that justifies this fear to some extent. 'Enthusiasts' were sometimes people who had plenty of heat but not too much light. They got all excited about minor things. Fanatics are enthusiastic, but such enthusiasm can sometimes lead to stupidity or even violence. Paul said before he was a Christian he was zealous. But his zeal was misdirected: he persecuted the church.

W. B. Yeats in his poem 'The Second Coming' says 'the best lack all conviction' while 'the worst are full of passionate intensity'. We must search for the dividing line between enthusiasm and fanaticism — being inspired by God or the devil. A person without judgment is like a car without brakes; but a person without enthusiasm is like a car without a motor.

The Presbyterian scholar and preacher James Stewart once said: 'The supreme need of the church is the same in the twentieth century as in the first: it is people on fire for Christ'.

O Thou who camest from above
The pure celestial fire to impart,
Kindle a flame of sacred love,
On the mean altar of my heart!
A cold church is like cold butter: it doesn't spread very easily.

Discuss: 'Enthusiasm is more caught than taught.' How true is this?

14

Leaders who love goodness

Barnabas was a 'good man' (Acts 11:24), and when churches are led by people who love goodness (rather than power, for example), those churches are healthy. Goodness is one of the fruits of the Holy Spirit (Galatians 5:22). It is kindness at work, so the word is sometimes translated 'generosity.' The word for goodness (*agathosune*) is not found in secular Greek. Graeco-Roman philosophers sometimes commended selfless generosity, but it was not a highly significant virtue for them.

Christian goodness is embodied in Jesus Christ. The best of the saints, says Sangster, have a peculiar kind of goodness.

It unconsciously proclaims itself. One feels it as an aura around its possessor. It is incandescent (which is why artists have painted halos around saints). It is essential goodness: goodness 'in the inward parts'. Its radiations are so powerful that it may be doubted whether anyone could be near it and quite unaware of it ... The saints are unconscious of it themselves. Blissfully unaware of the impression they make, they move on their way reminding people of Jesus Christ.[1]

How do you get to be like this? When you live closely with another you tend to be greatly influenced by that one. Good Christians are Christ-centred. George Muller, to whom God gave thousands of orphans and more than a million pounds, was asked his spiritual secret.

There was a day when I died, utterly died, died to George Muller, his opinions, preferences, tastes and will; died to the world, its approval or censure; died to the approval or blame even of my brethren and friends and, since then, I have studied only to show myself approved unto God.

So goodness is much more than 'doing good things', obeying the law, or helping others now and then. You can keep a rigid moral code and be a Pharisee. The person who says 'I'm as good as the next person' isn't good. The saints don't compare themselves with the next person but with Christ. Their goodness is not defensive or self-serving. The first thought of saints is never themselves. The centre of the saint's life is the Lord. Their goodness is a gift from God, nurtured by love, not something they've done themselves by hard effort.

Good people are guileless. They live simply. They tend to have a naive indifference to what others hold dearly — money or reputation, for example. Life is complex for those who want more money or a better position: they have to bother constantly about 'playing their cards right', and so the interior life suffers.

For the saint, says Sangster, the centre of life has shifted from self to Christ. Being assured of God's will the saint simply accepts it. Suffering, set back, misunderstanding ... the saint takes them all: they are God's agents to shape and purge one's soul. Each new day is greeted with childlike wonder, because of the deep knowledge that we are surrounded by Infinite Wisdom and Infinite Love.

Hence, the saint is without guile and does not aim to 'use' you, as so many use their friends. The saint loves you — and for yourself alone. The saint is not mentally fitting you into his or her scheme — they have none. Loving you with a God-like love, the saint has but one thought — how to help you. The saint's luminous eyes rest on your face and you know he or she is your servant. The love God gives the saint is 'always slow to expose, always eager to believe the best, always hopeful, always patient' (1 Corinthians 13:7 *Moffat*).[2]

This great virtue is forged in the personal, private disciplines of devotion, and is also corporate: each of us is helped by others in our quest for holiness and goodness, and we are meant to spread this virtue around (Romans 15:14; Ephesians 5:9; 2 Thessalonians 1:11).

If there is any mark of 'life' in a church, surely it is goodness.

Discuss: How do 'good' people get to be that way?

Further Reading: 'Goodness', by H. P. Owen, in John Macquarrie, (ed.) *A Dictionary of Christian Ethics.* London: SCM, 1967, pp. 137–9. W. E. Sangster. *The Pure in Heart.* London: Epworth, 1954 (out-of-print, but worth a search in second-hand bookshops).

NOTES

1 W. E. Sangster, *The Pure in Heart: A Study in Christian Sanctity* (London: Epworth, 1954), p. 140.

2 ibid., p. 146.

15

How to be filled with the Holy Spirit

In his famous sermon *The Wind of the Spirit* (Victory Press, Eastbourne, 1975), James Stewart notes that one of the marks of the Spirit's moving amongst us is that 'we hear the sound thereof'.
> This is the indisputable evidence of the Spirit. When the wind is blowing, it makes its presence felt. You hear its sound ... When the Spirit of God stirs up a church or an individual or a community, there are palpable evidences of his working. Even the unbeliever becomes aware that something is going on. The effects can be seen. The sound can be heard ... The hard supercilious pagan world of Greece and Rome professed itself indifferent to the gospel; but it could not deny that wherever Christ's people went strange things kept happening ... The world, says the Book of Acts, saw the evidences: it 'took knowledge of them that they had been with Jesus'.[1]

Notice that Luke equates being 'filled with the Spirit' with moral qualities, goodness and faith. Being 'Spirit-filled' does not refer to a special experience as such, although we ought to be open to whatever experiences of the Spirit the Lord has for us. Sometimes, in Acts, people spoke in tongues when 'filled with the Spirit'; but Acts often speaks of people filled with the Spirit with no reference, explicit or implicit, to tongues (Acts 4:8, 31; 6:3, 5; 7:55; 9:17; 11:24;

13:9, 52). 'If being Spirit-filled without glossolalia was the lot of some, then, it may be God's path for some now.'[2]

However, you can't be 'Spirit-filled' without exhibiting fruits of the Spirit such as goodness and faith. They are the inevitable proofs of the Spirit's presence in our lives. So the term 'Spirit-filled' ought to be used to describe Christian character rather than a spiritual experience. Remember — being 'Spirit-filled' is to be filled with God himself! God is the 'Spirit of holiness'.

'Do not get drunk with wine, which will only ruin you; instead, be filled with the Spirit' (Ephesians 5:18). How can I be filled with the Holy Spirit? Paul in this text notes three things. First a comparison: being filled with the Holy Spirit is something like being drunk with wine. When intoxicated you lose your inhibitions, you can talk more freely; so the Holy Spirit removes our fear and gives us a new freedom, boldness and power.

Then by way of contrast: whereas drunkenness makes us lose control the Spirit helps us to be self-controlled; the drunken person is undisciplined, the spiritual person disciplined; drunkenness makes us foolish, the Spirit makes us wise. And note Paul's command: 'Go on being filled with the Spirit' the Greek language has it, literally. It's not an option, but a command.

So being filled with the Spirit is something you choose to ask God to do: it's a matter of the will. God does this work in you (Philippians 1:11) but you are not merely passive: your human personality is actively yielding to the Divine Personality (Philippians 2:12, 13). You must want above anything else to surrender to the Spirit — hungering and thirsting to do what God wants (Matthew 5:6), i.e. to be filled with the Spirit rather than be filled with self. Confess your sins, so that you can be forgiven and cleansed (1 John 1:7).

If a vessel is to be filled with something, it must be emptied of what is already there: so if there is anything in your life which displaces the Spirit you must be willing for God to empty you of these things, so you can become 'poor in spirit' (Matthew 5:3). You must renounce the 'world, the flesh and the devil'. And all this is done with the same faith by which you received the Spirit in the first place, when you became a Christian (Mark 11:24).

For some, the Spirit comes upon them in an experience of power, love and deep emotion. With others, it is a quiet, determined, almost matter-of-fact transaction. The great saints in the past experienced the Spirit in many and varied ways. The reality of the Spirit's fullness is a matter of faith, and then discipline.

Derek Prince tells of two neighbours, one with a beautiful garden, the next overgrown with weeds. The first watered his flowers with a watering can, laboriously and regularly. The other had a hose and a powerful water supply, but was slack, and undisciplined. The question is not your experience of the Spirit in the past, but are you living a disciplined, Spirit-controlled life in the present?

Should I ask someone to lay hands on me to receive the fullness of the Spirit? Why not? Such 'laying on of hands' to receive God's gifts happened in the biblical stories. Just make sure the hands laid on you belong to someone filled with goodness and faith. Being filled with the Spirit is not a sideshow act!

As we read the book of Acts, being filled with the Spirit was a very definite experience (see 2:4, 4:8, 31, 6:3–5, 9:17, 11:24). It wasn't just for leaders but for everyone (Acts 2:4, cf. 2:39; 13:52). Being filled with the Spirit enables us to live a God-honouring life rather than one serving our own desires (Galatians 5:16). Being filled with the Spirit gives us power for service and witness (Acts 1:8). Jesus said ask, seek, knock; the Father wants to give the Holy Spirit to all who ask him (Luke 11:13).

A Prayer: 'Spirit of the living God, fall afresh on me: break me, melt me, mould me, fill me . . .'

Further Reading: David Watson. *One in the Spirit.* London: Hodder & Stoughton, 1975; *I Believe in the Church.* London: Hodder & Stoughton, 1978.

NOTES

1. James S. Stewart, *The Wind of the Spirit* (Eastbourne: Victory Press, 1975), pp. 14–15.
2 J. I. Packer, *Keep in Step with the Spirit* (Leicester: IVP, 1984), pp. 205–6.

16

The (corporate) just shall live by faith

Churches do not come alive accidentally: usually someone has a vision that gets translated into reality. Vision = imagination + faith. Vision is the capacity to see possibilities. The visionary leader believes opportunities are everywhere; without vision, another will be overcome by problems or obstacles, and succumb to complacency and despair. An optimist sees an opportunity in every problem; a pessimist sees a problem in every opportunity.

When twelve spies were sent into the Promised Land, two of them — Joshua and Caleb — believed it was a good land and could be occupied immediately. The other ten reported the land was infertile and full of giants: 'We felt as small as grasshoppers, and that is how we must have looked to them' (Numbers 13:33). The same country can be seen so differently depending on whether you are on the mountain of faith or in the valley of doubt and pessimism. G. K. Chesterton was right when he said that a positive challenge is a difficulty rightly understood.

Planning and decision making that leave nothing to trust in God is hardly Christian. The Holy Spirit gives the 'gift of faith' to the church (1 Corinthians 12:9) to bring moral and spiritual courage, strengthen God's people, and convince unbelievers of God's presence among his people, particularly when this gift effects 'impossible' signs and wonders (Matthew 17:19–20). This is 'fourth dimension faith' as I heard Paul Yonggi Cho, pastor of the world's largest church in Seoul, Korea, describe it.

In that same talk Dr Cho said 'Your worst enemies are your negative thoughts'. 'If your mind is negatively charged, spiritual power will never flow through you.' 'Like attracts like; optimism is contagious; an optimistic person attracts other optimistic persons, to help build the church to the greater glory of God.'

But leaders with vision will also inherit colleagues who prefer stability and 'more-of-the-same' to growth and challenge. I heard Lyle Schaller make this astonishing comment: 'Most people come to church meetings with one unspoken agenda: don't do anything to challenge my comfortable life'! 'Live' churches tend to have leaders who are disturbing risk takers; who ask 'why not?'; who make faith decisions — 'What does God want us to do?' — rather than 'Can we afford it?' They oughtn't to ignore traditions or precedents or budget projections; they are guided, rather than ruled by them.

Having this sort of vision will show up the problems and inertia very early. Although the faith-filled leader will redefine problems as opportunities, he or she will still need to plan to budget a considerable portion of time for trouble-shooting and problem-solving.

Earlier (chapter 7) we talked about *'fides'* faith, God's gift to anyone, Christian or not. In Denis Waitley's best-seller *Seeds of Greatness*, his seventh 'best-kept secret of total success' is: 'Life is a self-fulfilling prophecy; you won't necessarily get what you want in life, but in the long run you will usually get what you expect'.[1] The positive power of this sort of faith is available to everyone.

Dom Helder Camara, the archbishop persecuted by the Brazilian authorities for taking sides with the poor, has written a beautiful book of poems and verses, *A Thousand Reasons for Living*. Here's one: I like the sort of birds
that fall in love with
stars and drop, worn out
from trying to catch their light.[2]

Henry Ford said, 'Think you can; think you can't. Either way you'll be right!' Another wise person said, 'Things turn out best for folks who make the best of the way things turn out'. The 'corporate just' shall live by faith!

NOTES

1 Denis Waitley, *Seeds of Greatness* (New Jersey: Revell, 1983), p. 148.

2 Dom Helder Camara, *A Thousand Reasons for Living* (London: Darton Longman and Todd, 1984), p. 56.

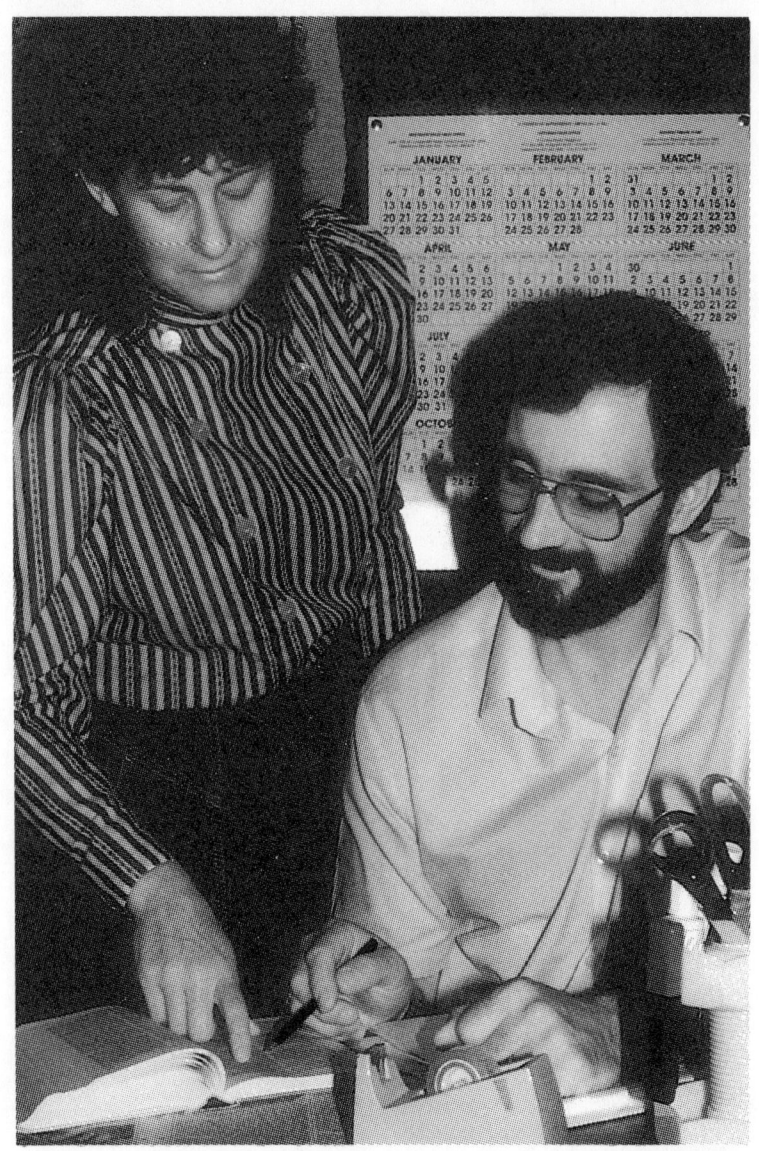

Photo: Kelvin Young

17

Team ministries

Barnabas acted immediately to add Paul to the 'pastoral team' (Acts 11:25). We don't read of a special meeting of the church (with three Sundays' notice) and a treasurer's report before Barnabas took this action. It was apparently assumed that if you're going to encourage the rapid spiritual growth of new converts you have to find people quickly to disciple them.

Here's another common component of dynamic churches: they add full- or half-time 'ministers' to their leadership team, usually before they can 'afford' to, thus building momentum into growth of the church's ministries. Note that we put 'ministers' in quotation marks: all Christians are ministers, but some are set apart from their secular callings to do special tasks among God's people. They are usually persons who are 'reproducers', who can disciple others in the faith and multiply the number of growing Christians in the church. Such leaders use their special gifts to train, equip others for ministry (Ephesians 4:12).

There is now quite a large amount of experience about how team ministries function. Here's a summary of this accumulated wisdom:

- Every team needs a captain. Team leaders empower the other team members to actualise their potential in ministry. Their role is not to delegate uncongenial jobs, or monopolise ministry tasks simply because they are the team leader; that's sometimes a sign of insecurity. For example, if a senior pastor thinks that because he/she is senior pastor they should be the only preacher or perform all baptisms, that's a pretty shaky proposition: Jesus and Paul delegated ministry tasks to others. A small piece of research I did in one Australian denomination found that when a two member pastoral team experienced tension, this was often caused by the senior pastor being jealous of the kudos directed towards the associate. The senior pastor may have been there first, had a sense of 'ownership' in the church, and found it difficult to 'share the glory' with a (gifted) other.

• Members of pastoral teams should meet regularly for fellowship, discussion of major matters relating to the church, and prayer — say, two hours once a week. And then go on a retreat for one or two days, once or twice a year.

When team members function harmoniously they energise one another. There is richness in their diversity, and the whole group has an impact on the church community much greater than the sum of its parts. Other pairs of eyes are watching for landmines one person alone may step on. Other pairs of ears are listening for feedback that may not come to a solo pastor.

• Harmony in a leadership team is only maintained if none of them cares too much who gets the glory for a job well done. However, encourage one another, and gently suggest improvements if something can be done better. Usually team members will be functioning within the areas of their own giftedness anyway, so they will receive regular 'strokes' from the congregation for their performance.

• Team members ought to be involved in the selection process for additions to the team. When they are thrown together by another body, we usually have a recipe for disaster. Should the associates resign when the senior pastor does? Not necessarily, in my view (but read Schaller's book for another opinion on this vexed question) — provided those remaining have a strong input in the selection of the new senior pastor. Conversely, should the new appointee insist on the resignations of the existing team? Again, in my view, only in rare circumstances. Americans sometimes regard the senior pastor as 'executive director' of the church who hires and fires his own staff. Most western churches have a more 'collegial' arrangement, except in some Pentecostal groups where the senior pastor is viewed as a sort of 'patriarch'.

• New team members ought to be invited to write their own 'ministry description' within the broad guidelines of their invited calling. This (one page) document would then be submitted to the call committee, and to the church for their approval. Don't be too

legalistic: hopefully pastors grow in their experience and may be redirected to a new field of ministry after a time. Such ministry descriptions ought to include a statement about ministry at home (my own view is that no pastor needs to be out of his or her home more than 3-4 evenings per week); and also time for study and preparation, as well as, say, two weeks' study leave each year.
• Probably all the ministry team ought to have regular visibility in the church's worship services, ministering according to their gifts. As hinted above, that means team members preach according to their giftedness. Preaching is a highly prized area of ministry: it's always near the top of most pastors' favoured occupations. When I entered the Baptist ministry, a godly old evangelist said, 'Preachers are peacocks — watch it!' Unfortunately he was mostly right.

Who determines who preaches how often, and when? My suggestion is that the preachers ought to trust their fellow elders and team members as a larger group. For example, on your church leaders' retreats, draw up a grid of the services, a hypothetical ten Sundays, ask each person to nominate who should preach when (including non-team church members and visiting preachers), and design a roster from the averages. This allows preachers to be subject to the leadership of the church: I like that. After all, our leaders have to suffer our pulpit performances, and they may have a more objective assessment of our value as preachers or teachers. They also receive more objective feedback from rank-and-file church members. Woe to the preacher who believes too readily the kind comments from his favourite old ladies!
• A ministry support team, including secretaries and administrators, ought to be put in place early. In most churches there's a large pool of unused talent waiting to be employed which, financially, would cost the church little or nothing: early retirees, the unemployed, some on invalid pensions, spouses of the well employed who do not need to work at a salaried job. What should they do in the church? The short answer: whatever they're gifted to do! But never — I repeat, never — call for volunteers for key jobs, particularly those that call for a high degree of confidentiality.
• What positions should be filled first? That depends on four factors: the culture in which the church exists, ministry needs within the church community, opportunities in the church's mission area, and the spiritual gifts of those available (mostly within the church body) for ministry. In western middle-class churches, I would suggest, as a rough guide, the following: senior pastor, part-time secretary (voluntary in a very small church, but paid as early as possible), then youth pastor or small group facilitator, then make the secretary full-time, then evangelist, children's worker,

community ministries pastor or music director. The first three pastoral positions are filled by 'reproducers' — persons who train others for ministry; that's most important. If your church has a large body of older people who expect regular pastoral visitation by an 'ordained' minister, perhaps appoint a semi-retired pastor for this task.

Another good idea: look for a trained counsellor, who may operate on a pay-as-you-can fee basis. (Senior pastors who spend a lot of time in continuous pastoral counselling rarely lead growing churches.) Add youth leaders as full- or part-time staff workers, perhaps on a team support basis. There are literally hundreds of young people waiting for a challenge like this: ask organisations like Youth With a Mission or Young Life which have trained thousands of them partly because local churches were slow to realise their potential.

- If Barnabas added Saul to his pastoral team so early, how did they afford it financially? Saul was a tent maker, and we know he used that occupation to support himself. That could be part of the answer: a pastor or youth leader working part-time, and being supported as well by the church.

But there are other ways. Here are two experiences from my own pastoral history. At Narwee Baptist Church in Sydney, during the late 1960s, I was their part-time student pastor. Many young people became Christians, so my wife Jan and I prayed about adding a youth pastor to our church's staff. The church had taken a leap of faith to call us: they had single student pastors before, and had to increase their pastoral stipend and find a house for us. So adding more staff was probably not on their agenda.

Jan and I decided to double our tithe, then started contacting people who might join us in this commitment: first, parents with both teenagers and a good income, then other teenagers' parents, then people without kids but with good jobs, then the young people themselves. Our question: will you join us in pledging extra finance for just one year — believing that the person invited will disciple other young people, who'll bring their money with them, and after one year be virtually self-supporting?! One year's stipend plus house plus car were pledged in 24 hours. Dave Kendall, an American, who is now the Bible Society's youth specialist in New South Wales joined our church, and the momentum began: this church now has four full-time pastors, plus office staff.

At Blackburn Baptist Church in Victoria we did a similar thing when actor/singer Robert Colman was added to our church staff to engage in a ministry of evangelism and music.

- Some notes on male/female teams: women and men provide

complementary ministries if they are to work well together. Perhaps every church needs a mother figure. Men will have to learn to allow women to be both feminine and achieving. Women will permit men to be risk takers. However, men often define themselves in terms of their work accomplishments: so loss of job equals loss of identity. They may be tempted to see their primary role as a professional person. Women on the other hand tend to add any new role to existing ones. They become workaholics for another reason: to prove their worth in the first modern generation to allow them to be leaders.

So expect to add to your pastoral staff. You must sow seeds to get a harvest. A population explosion will only happen if you multiply the reproducers!

Finally, note this important observation:

Your team, empowered and directed by God in Christ, becomes a model in the parish for harmonious relationships and effective ministry, working together, supporting each other, urgently sharing the gospel, caring for others, admitting mistakes and confessing sins, forgiving and giving. Your team's example catches on contagiously and infectiously. God grips the parish through you so that the Word comes alive in ministry. The whole parish operates as his team for the community and for the world.[1]

Further Reading: Lyle Schaller. *The Multiple Staff and the Larger Church.* Nashville: Abingdon, 1980; Ervin Henkelmann and Stephen Carter. *How to Develop a Team Ministry and Make it Work.* St Louis: Concordia, 1985; Norman Wegmeyer. *Strengthening the Multiple Staff.* Minneapolis: Augsburg Publishing House, 1982; Harold Westing. *Multiple Church Staff Handbook.* Grand Rapids Michigan: Kregel Publications, 1985.

NOTES

1 Ervin Henkelmann and Stephen Carter, *How to Develop a Team Ministry and Make it Work* (St Louis: Concordia, 1985), p. 90.

18

Leadership selection: move with the movers!

Sometimes unlikely people make the best leaders. Would you have chosen the impetuous Peter or the quisling Matthew? Or Saul of Tarsus, implicated in the persecution and murder of Christians? It's the nature of most churches and denominations to 'play it safe' and choose people who are 'like us'. They thereby ignore the great potential that often resides in people who may be creatively unconventional! Fortunately Barnabas was big enough to see Saul's potential where others couldn't, and the church at Antioch benefited from his significant evangelistic and teaching gifts.

What is leadership? Experts aren't entirely sure. One writes: 'There are many theories and more than a hundred definitions of leadership'. And another: 'Leadership is one of the most observed and least understood phenomena on earth'.

Leaders are people who get things done through others (who also want those things to get done). There are three kinds of human beings: those who make things happen, those who watch things happen, and those who wonder what happened! Leaders make things happen!

All human groups need leaders. Effective leaders know where

they're going: they have strong beliefs and values. Good leaders exude and inspire confidence, are willing to take risks and make sacrifices. Good leaders have one key aim: to be a servant to maximise others' potentials for the good of the whole enterprise. Good leaders can verbalise their strategic vision for the organisation. They are effective communicators, moulding people's ideas. That's the difference between a political leader and a statesman: the first follows public opinion; statesmen (and women) shape it.

So smart leaders will know what their colleagues are thinking: this they learn through feedback. And they will never be too far in front or behind the group they're leading. Sometimes a leader will have to surrender a cherished goal because the group isn't yet ready to follow. Here's a personal example. Baptists around the world are divided over the question of 'closed' versus 'open' membership. My strong belief as the senior pastor in one church was (and still is) that we ought to welcome into the membership of our church all whom the Lord has accepted into his church, and let people sort out the issue of the mode and timing of baptism for themselves. Some of our leaders said this wasn't 'Baptist': weren't all the people in the New Testament baptised knowingly as believers? Well, yes, I said, that's my own position too but haven't Baptists also strongly held the view that each of us ought to be free to be guided by the Holy Spirit in our study of the Scriptures? And didn't Jesus say, 'It's acceptance of others I want, not ordinances' (Matthew 9:13). But those ordinances came from God: is Jesus saying people matter more than laws . . . ? And so on. But I failed to convince some of them, and made a tactical retreat from the issue: perhaps I'm 'chicken' but I wasn't ready to be martyred (or create division in the church) over that one. As one truism puts it, a leader will realise that the unintended effects of any policy change are apt to be larger and more lasting than the intended effects.

When leaders are decisive this will generate opposition. That's why they're leaders: others have not (yet) been given their gift of vision. If you want approval badly, or a life free of pressure, don't be a leader. Leadership requires courage: it involves risk tasking and possibly ridicule, opposition or rejection. 'Courage' comes from the French word for 'heart' — coeur — and means simply your heart's in it! Have you heard the old story of the mule standing in the centre of a circle of hay? The mule was hungry, but there was no wind: he could not smell the fragrance of the hay. But he could see it: he was surrounded by equally attractive goals. He stayed in the centre and starved to death. Too many church leaders are indecisive like that.

Other capacities a leader will need include teachability, a facility for uniting people together, and hard, hard work! The life of a leader was never meant to be easy!

What about leadership style? In all cultures, the leader must operate in ways acceptable to the group (or else organise armed guards to eliminate opposition!). Authoritarian leaders (the 'tells' style) are sometimes acceptable where people are insecure or immature. They often get things done quickly and efficiently, but when the group matures there'll be hostility, competitiveness, scapegoating, and discontent. Consensual leaders ('sells' style) seek the group's approval, and when they get it there's more harmony, teamwork and satisfaction, and, eventually, increasing productivity. Laissez-faire leaders have an 'in basket' management style. Their program is determined by whatever comes along. Initiatives come from elsewhere or not at all, and the group gets frustrated when they realise they're not going anywhere.

Leaders get things done through other people in four stages: planning (forecasting opportunities, spelling out objectives, outlining the steps and time limits to reach those objectives), organising (developing a structure within which groups can work effectively, delegating authority and responsibility to other leaders, promoting teamwork), leading (making good decisions, communicating these, motivating and training people), and controlling (developing measures of performance, evaluating results, and making 'course corrections').

One word in the paragraph above is most important: motivation. Developing a climate where church people are highly motivated to serve the Lord and other people is a challenge for leaders. People are highly motivated when (1) they know they are loved, (2) they are invited to do a job commensurate with their gifts, only a little more stretching, (3) they are adequately trained, (4) they know precisely what they are to do, by when, with what resources to help, and (5) their psychological needs are met (e.g., encouragement, security, socialising, fulfilment when a job's well done and appreciated, etc.). Some pastors and church leaders say these factors shouldn't be important: we should serve the Lord altruistically, from a motive of love alone. Well, yes, in heaven we will all do that! Surveys show most pastors 'enjoy' preaching more than anything else. One said: 'Preaching's the only thing I do that is not at the mercy of petty bureaucrats!' So it's not wrong to allow people in the church to do what they enjoy doing either. Motivation then becomes a lot easier.

'But Rowland', pastors often say to me, 'the blighters in our church won't work!' Douglas McGregor's 'theory x and theory y' have helped me at this point. According to 'theory x' management, thinking people hate work and will avoid it if they can, so they must be coerced, controlled, directed, or threatened to get anything done. 'Theory y' leaders believe work is as natural as play or rest, and workers will be highly motivated to work towards goals to which they are committed: they will be self-directing and will seek and accept responsibility; imagination, ingenuity, and creativity are widely not narrowly distributed among the population. Pastor, the blighters will work, if all the above factors are noted!

Are leaders born or made? Probably both. There's an indefinable charismatic quality about outstanding leaders. However, the Lord promises wisdom to all of us: the leadership equation is godly wisdom (James 1:5) + enthusiasm (1 Peter 5:2) + faith (Hebrews 13:7) + hard work (1 Thessalonians 5:12,13).

Discuss: How do the leadership styles mentioned above apply to your church? Look at the leaders cited in Hebrews 11: they were a varied lot, but matched the occasion into which they were called. What lessons are there for us? Study the leadership qualities in 1 Timothy 3. What do these mean in our culture?

Further Reading: Gerard Egan. *Change Agent Skills in Helping and Human Service Settings.* California: Brooks/Cole, 1985 (especially chapter 11 'Leadership'); J. M. Burns. *Leadership.* New York: Harper & Row, 1978; J. Oswald Sanders. *Spiritual Leadership.* Chicago: Moody Press, 1967; Ted W. Engstrom and Edward R. Dayton. *The Art of Management for Christian Leaders.* Waco: Word, 1979, and *Strategy for Leadership.* New Jersey: Fleming H. Revell, 1979; R. Wolff. *Man at the Top.* London: Tyndale, 1970; Lawrence O. Richards and Clyde Hoeldtke. *A Theology of Church Leadership.* Grand Rapids: Zondervan, 1980; Peter Wagner. *Leading Your Church to Growth.* Ventura: Regal, 1984.

19

The teaching ministry of the church

'If anything is worth doing, it is worth telling someone how to do it well.'

One church is 'loaded' with highly committed, talented workers, another is struggling to keep its doors open: and they're side by side in the same suburb or town. Why? The secret is often in the way those highly motivated church members are taught.

How do we mature in our faith and life? How do we develop a sensitive Christian conscience, a strong desire to live obediently to the Word of God, a love for Bible study and prayer, a dedicated commitment to ministries of evangelism, mercy and justice? A discussion of teaching must work backwards from these questions.

When asked 'What or who were the formative influences in your life?' most people name a parent or teacher. U.S. professor of the year in 1983, Peter Beidler, says that he teaches because he sees people grow and change in front of his eyes. He claims that being a teacher is like being present at creation, when the clay begins to breathe. For him, nothing is more exciting than being nearby when the breathing begins ... he teaches because, being around people who are beginning to breathe, he occasionally finds himself catching his breath with them.[1]

Paul and Barnabas majored on teaching (Acts 11:26). The church at Antioch had a list of their teachers (Acts 13:1): does yours? The religion of Israel was a teaching religion (see e.g. Exodus 18:20, Deuteronomy 6:1): the law of Moses was first a lesson, then a command. Jesus was a rabbi, a teacher (e.g. Mark 1:38), and commanded his followers to go into the world and teach all nations (Matthew 28:19-20). The early Christian churches took seriously the function of teaching (Acts 13:1, 1 Corinthians 12:28, Ephesians 4:11, 2 Timothy 1:11). Paul later describes the teaching-learning process in this summary: 'All you have learned by participation in the church's life, by listening, by watching my example; put this now into practice' (Philippians 4:9).

The purpose of Timothy's teaching, Paul says, is to 'arouse the love that comes from a pure heart, a clear conscience, and a genuine faith' (1 Timothy 1:5). 'Bible teaching' is therefore much more than a 'jug to mug' approach: it's meant to produce better behaved rather than merely better informed Christians. Christian leaders should be able, or apt to teach (1 Timothy 3:2).

If you could choose one verb to describe what the pastor/s do in your church, would it be 'teaching'? In churches battling to survive, the leaders spend their time 'oiling the church's machinery' or 'keeping the people happy' through routine visitation (so called 'maintenance' ministries). But where the 'pastor-teachers' (Ephesians 4:11) take their teaching role seriously, they use many means to encourage their people to mature in the faith, serve others, and become 'reproducers'. Pastoring and teaching go together: we don't teach theory, we teach persons. The best teachers love those they instruct, model what they teach ('truthing it in love' as Paul puts it in Ephesians 4:15), are enthusiastic, hard working and systematic in their preparation, and always assume their students will teach others (2 Timothy 2:2).

Teaching and preaching also belong together. The New Testament writers drew a distinction between *kerygma* (proclamation by a herald) and *didache* (teaching, instruction). Preaching addresses our unbelief (urging a response to the word of God), teaching our ignorance (encouraging a learner to understand the Christian faith). Preaching mainly addresses the will, teaching the mind. Of course preaching without teaching can be propaganda: bypassing people's minds to get them to make a commitment they don't fully understand. And teaching without persuasion can be dry, sterile dogma.

Christian teaching moves through four stages: listening to the Word, reflecting on the Word, 'uttering' the Word, and 'doing' the Word. Listening to and reflecting on the Word is best done in uninterrupted silence: so a sign will go on the door, the telephone answering machine is switched on, and we will create a 'desert'. As one of my pastor-mentors put it: if you take your teaching ministry seriously you'll take down the sign 'Office' and put up 'Study'! Uttering is done through word (what we say), deed (what we do) and sign (what God does to corroborate his word and works through ours). So the teacher's life must be congruent with his or her teaching; and we'll be open to the power of God, as we noted in chapter 6.

Paulo Freire is perhaps this century's most outstanding teacher. In his *Pedagogy of the Oppressed*, he attacks conventional education for its 'banking' approach: the teacher knows and the student learns; information is put by the teacher into the head of the student — so the teacher talks and the student listens; the teacher is the active, the student the passive part of the process; the teacher has authority and the student must submit. Freire is not suggesting that students 'do their own thing', but that teachers and taught become transformed together in the process of transforming the world. Words are used to understand experience and reality. The result is 'conscientisation' — a recognition of one's dignity and worth and a movement towards change in society to enhance others' dignity and worth.[2]

Building on this approach, Henri Nouwen draws an important distinction between 'violent' and 'redemptive' models of teaching. Teaching as a violent process is competitive (knowledge is property to be defended rather than a gift to be shared); unilateral (from 'strong teacher' to 'weak student'); and alienating (teachers belong to a different world to that of the students). Redemptive teaching is evocative (drawing out others' potentials); bilateral (teachers and students learn together, and from each other); and actualising (envisaging the building of a better world).[3]

The teaching process will be 'dialogical',[4] inductive and deductive, propositional and relational, doctrinal and life-centred, from the pulpit, in classes, in small groups, and one-to-one. Every church that's alive has a bookstall (positioned where people will fall over it!); and an audio and video cassette library. Perhaps small group studies can be related to the whole church's theme for the week, where the sermon is followed up by discussion. (That's better than the reverse order: experience shows too many will come with their exegetical — and critical — minds made up to truly hear the voice of the Lord in the preaching.)

Teaching happens from the pulpit; in preparation for marriage; in membership classes; and training for elders, deacons, home visitors, people helpers, Sunday school teachers, etc. Some churches have 'Training Days' or special mid-week options offering classes on everything ranging from leading singing to an overview of church history to a Christian reaction to high school English texts. Whatever your people want to learn — find a teacher and form a 'learning exchange'. Adult education classes are proliferating in their thousands in Western cities and towns these days: why doesn't your church offer some? And don't forget to run a course on English for newcomers from other lands, perhaps using the *Good News Bible* as your text.

Teaching children

A newspaper columnist writes:

> Not one of Australia's 100,000 State school teachers, or the 40,000 currently training, was selected because of personal qualities. Each was chosen as a two legged set of percentages ... What this means is that we do not care much what happens in our schools ... Teachers should be chosen on grounds of commitment, intelligence, creativity and empathetic understanding of other persons, rather than merely on the basis of examination results.

The same can be said of our universities, and, sometimes our theological halls and churches.

Wise old Socrates used to say that if he could get to the highest point in Athens he would lift up his voice and cry: 'What mean you, fellow citizens, that scrape every stone to get wealth together and take so little care of your children to whom one day you must relinquish all?'

I still believe in Sunday schools, but only in churches where the adults are learners too. The most powerful influence on a child is an adult who obviously loves the Lord. As I once heard Lyle Schaller say 'In every church meeting there are children taking notes!'

We desperately need teachers who are exciting, interesting and creative. Pedagogy, said someone, is more an art than a science. I agree. If we are forced to make a choice, give me a shallow teacher who teaches with enthusiasm and zest, over another who may be scholarly but boring! Teachers of children should understand the kids' home situations and interests. Good teachers will control by presence rather than by threats; they will work hard to prepare an interesting lesson; they're able to adapt themselves to different situations (as when a kid is angry or grieving or curious); they will do interesting things with their class outside lesson time; and they will have a sense of humour. They will vary their approach (videos, team teaching, object lessons). Sunday school teachers should not be chosen because they've outgrown the children's classes, or because there's nothing much else in the church for them to do. It would be better to have fewer teachers than poor, untrained ones. Teachers of children are *in loco parentis*: a high responsibility. A university professor gave up his work among young adults to teach boys. When asked for a reason he said: 'If you were to write your name on brick so that it would remain, would you write it before or after it was baked?'

And adults

Many Christians unfortunately view Sunday school as 'nice for the kids'. This reminds me of a rabbi's lament about 'pediatric Judaism' in his religion: the view that training stops when the child has received his Bar Mitzvah. Indeed the Jewish Talmud says that in the world to come we'll be asked three questions: 'Did you buy and sell in good faith? Did you have a set time for study? Did you raise a family?' Let us encourage everyone in the church to be a student, a learner, a grower, forever.

Children and youth are important, but it's useful to recall Jesus didn't start a youth movement. The church was started by adults; it was organised by adults; and throughout the world the church is growing to the extent that it is reaching out to adults. When heads of families make a commitment to Christ, you're more likely to win the whole family.

Adults aren't all the same. There is a burgeoning literature now seeking to map adult life-cycles.[5] John Claypool writes: 'If adolescence is the most intense stage along the way, I would say adulthood is the most demanding. Not only is it long, it also involves so many different challenges simultaneously'. He then notes Gail Sheehy's phrase 'concomitant growth': adults grow concurrently in three areas: vocation, relationships with one's 'significant others' and one's own unique selfhood.[6]

The first adult stage involves leaving the family (ages 16–22), where the young adult begins to leave youthful fantasies behind, establishes independence from the family, and establishes new friendships. Then there's a stage of reaching out towards others (23-28), with a search for personal identity with the help of an older 'mentor', an ability to develop intimacy, a time for togetherness in marriage and a devotion to conquering the world. Aged 29–34, the adult searches for stability: life looks more painful and difficult, so this is a time of intense questioning and reappraisal of life's values, and the setting of long range goals. The mid-life crisis period begins about 35–37: it's a time to face reality and one's mortality; one's marriage, personal priorities and values are reassessed. The way out of this turbulent stage, says Erikson, is through 'generativity' — nurturing, teaching and serving others. Life settles down in the late 40s through 50s. Money is less important; old values and family relationships reassume importance. Then, after the late 50s we experience the 'mellowing' stage, with adjustment to the ageing process, thoughts about the inevitable death of spouse, a tendency to avoid emotion-laden issues, and (at last!) parents aren't blamed for personal problems.

Another important way of looking at an adult group is in terms of the 'Baby Boomers': those born after World War II, between 1946 and 1964. They are the first adults to be raised on the mass media. Television, radio, rock music and computers have shaped the way they view reality. Some of them were Jesus freaks. In the U.S. there are over 76 million of them: about one-third of America. But they attend church only 6.2 times a year — less than half as often as Americans over 40. Yet George Gallup's research says 99% of young Americans are 'religious' in some sense, and 40 per cent say they're 'born again'. So they don't feel at home in the traditional church; it's boring, quite frankly. They don't like rigid structures, old fashioned music, or the church's conservative politics. One 33 year old pastor of a large church in Colorado said: 'The church is the last standing barrier between our generation and Jesus'.

Adults, like young people, want to be committed to something. They must be encouraged not to lose touch with their younger idealism. And they will make incredible sacrifices to grow towards maturity and ministry to others. I heard today of a Presbyterian church in Houston that conducts a Bible class for men at 6 a.m. Tuesday mornings, and is well attended by business and professional men.

The great danger for adults, as Erik Erikson and James Fowler have pointed out, is that they become permanently bogged down in a kind of restless social activism while the soul remains fixed in a sort of adolescent posture. The adult should move into middle years sufficiently full of spiritual and practical riches to endow others with the fruits of a reflective as well as actively well spent life. They can then move towards the 'shadow years' with the assurance that they have not squandered the gifts of God.

Now: Contact your denomination's headquarters and find out what training resources they offer for teachers in your church. Organise a training day with their help.

Suggested Reading: Locke E. Bowman. *Teaching Today: The Church's First Ministry.* Philadelphia: Westminster Press, 1980; James W. Fowler. *Becoming Adult, Becoming Christian: Adult Development and Christian Faith.* San Francisco: Harper and Row, 1984.

NOTES

1 See *Readers' Digest*, May 1987, pp. 91-93.

2 Paulo Freire, *Pedagogy of the Oppressed* (New York: Seabury, 1968).

3 Henri J. M. Nouwen, *Creative Ministry* (New York: Doubleday, 1978), pp. 5-14.

4 John R. W. Stott, *Between Two Worlds: The Art of Preaching in the Twentieth Century* (Michigan: Eerdmans, 1982), pp. 60ff.

5 Erik Erikson, *Insight and Responsibility* (New York: Norton, 1964); James Fowler, Stages of Faith (San Francisco: Harper & Row, 1981); Gerald O'Collins, *The Second Journey* (Melbourne: Dove, 1978); Evelyn and James Whitehead, *Christian Life Patterns* (New York: Doubleday, 1979).

6 John Claypool, *Stages: The Art of Living the Expected* (Waco: Word, 1977) p. 60.

20

Congregational participation in worship

Churches that are alive cannot contain the resources of the gospel for long. They want to reach out. And this church had a wonderfully balanced view of mission — involving evangelism and discipling, ministries of mercy, and a commitment to justice (Acts 11:27–30; 13:1–3). This missionary call came during a time of corporate worship. God made us for a purpose — and that purpose is worship. To affirm 'You, our Lord and God are worthy!' (Revelation 4:11) is the highest privilege we have, 'the most momentous, the most urgent, the most glorious action that can take place in human life' (Karl Barth). Worship is responding to the Greatest Worth of all — the living God himself.

So worship is not just a once-a-week affair. A little boy told his pastor he didn't pray every night because some nights he didn't want anything! When we think of worship as a one-day-only affair, we may be treating God as we would a lawyer or doctor, resorting to him when in trouble.

The earliest Christians had very little that was tangible beyond their worship assemblies, and travelling disciples who had been with Jesus of Nazareth and the risen Christ. They had no buildings, no sacred Christian book, no defined creed. What they had were burning convictions, and the loyalty and commitment that a possible knock on the door and impending death always engenders.

Some prophets arrived in Antioch, and an opportunity was given to one of them to bring their 'word from the Lord' to the church (Acts 11:27-28). At this point we ask: Is worship an event of the congregation or for the congregation? Who 'conducts' worship in your church? Pastors ('paid holy people') from the front? Or the whole congregation? Someone has said medieval worship centred on the altar; the Protestant Reformation moved it to the pulpit; today a renewed church sees the locus of worship within the congregation. 'Liturgy' literally means 'the work of the people'. The whole church is a priesthood (Hebrews 6). This does not, however, deny the validity of a set-apart leadership of the ministries of word, sacrament and pastoral care. As Thomas Oden put it, 'This requires committed and informed persons who have studied the tradition in more than a slapdash way as a serious lifelong pursuit and intentional vocational commitment and who have been set aside both by their inner sense of calling and by the outward action of the church'.[1]

These 'set-apart' persons are ordained to conduct (and in my view train others to conduct) worship, as a conductor of an orchestra facilitates beautiful symphonic sound. The orchestra plays the music, the conductor leads. If the leader is trying very hard to make me worship, I find worship difficult. But when they have given their best in preparation, and are themselves worshipping, I can only do likewise. The worship-leader is not the 'master of ceremonies' announcing each item on the list. He or she is also a worshipper. So we need more genius in putting a 'worship service' together that flows without too many 'promptings' from the worship-leader.

So if ever our corporate worship becomes a 'performance from the front' for the congregation-as-audience, it has degenerated into something less than our Lord intended. This set-up encourages a distance between the professional and laypeople. The latter are passive, expected to display feelings of awe, fear and trust towards the professional, who 'knows what's best'. Worship-leaders are not called to be entertainers. Worship is essentially reciprocal. The congregation should be encouraged to participate in worship in many ways, not the least of which are said (or in some liturgical churches, sung) prayer- and praise-responses, confession of sin, passing the peace, reading Scripture together, (in charismatic churches) singing in the Spirit, and (in some cultures) free form prayer said aloud by everyone at the same time.

Paul told the Corinthians when they came together for worship various ones would contribute in different ways (1 Corinthians 14:26). With gentle warm encouragement (it's probably better to err on the side of 'making haste slowly'), it's amazing how even conservative congregations will loosen up and lose their self-consciousness.

Every congregation should be exposed regularly to a two-track program of education about worship. The first track involves study. Run a course on worship throughout the established groups of the church, or combine them for a special 10-hour course over, say, five nights. Use World Vision's GRID on 'worship'[2] as a resource, or consult a recent book about worship. The pastor should be a 'key player' in formulating the content of the course, with the help of outside facilitators. Then, form up to three or four worship teams to be responsible for, say, three services each over the next 12 months. Each team member should have done the study course. The pastor (or preacher for the day) lists themes and scriptures, and each member of the team plans for one element of each service, the elements including: call to worship and invocation; confession and reconciliation; creed or covenant; prayer of thanksgiving; prayer of intercession; offertory prayer; benediction; hymns; a meaningful way of reading the Scripture. Each team has a coordinator who puts the whole service together with the pastor, and together they determine who will lead the various segments of the service. (Leaders should be given at least a week's notice.)[3]

Another important training opportunity is for pastors to prepare a sermon with a group from the church. They will then have a better understanding of homiletical principles, how to interpret the biblical text, and how to apply it to people's needs in preaching.

Movement

Up until the 14th century when pews were introduced, worshippers were free to move around. Then pews introduced a stiff symmetry and oppressive order into church buildings, discouraging the kind of physical involvement that could give somatic shape to inner feelings. Such movements have included forms of 'holy dancing' offered to the Lord or the 'holy kiss' offered to others. 'Today we are slowly beginning to re-learn how to love our bodies and live in our bodies ... Although we bring shame with our bodies, (not everybody is sufficiently in touch with their own sexuality to be ready for a dancer in leotards! RCC) we are learning no longer to be ashamed of our bodies. We are more ready than we have been in many generations to underline our praises with our bodies.'[4]

Art

Banners, audio-visual aids, symbols, images, and poetry, (for example T. S. Eliot's 'Ash Wednesday' or 'Choruses from the Rock') all enhance worship for some. Encourage some of your people to write poems.

Another way to involve the congregation more is through dialogical and interactive preaching. How that's done depends on the preacher's gifts and the hearers' culture. Remember the old educational adage: I learn by doing. I remember 90% of what I do, 75% of what I say, 50% of what I see, but only 10% of what I hear.

After the benediction

As I travel to different churches, I occasionally see something very beautiful going on in the congregation after the formal worship service has concluded. There are twos and threes everywhere in deep and meaningful conversation, perhaps praying together. It's one of the marks of a church that is really alive. In 'dead' churches they're out the door and off home pretty quickly!

Involving the congregation in worship is one of the hallmarks of a church that's alive. As we thus surrender to God, 'saying prayers' gives way to praying, 'going to church' to 'being the church'.

Discuss: (1) What for each of us is the most significant part of a worship service? Why is the order of service in your church set out the way it is? What changes would you suggest and why? (2) 'Christians are separated by their creeds and rituals but are united by their prayers and hymns.' How true is this? (3) 'We come to worship to give rather than to get.' Do we? Can we? How? (4) 'If the Queen should enter our worship place, we would all stand. If Jesus Christ entered, we would all fall to our knees.' Would we? (5) The weekends, with our 'four day weeks' and increasingly flexible work hours, are becoming times of exodus from the cities to 'weekenders' on the coast or elsewhere. How does this affect our worship habits? Could 'prayer breakfasts' or mid-week small groups take the place of traditional church worship?

Further Reading: Robert E. Webber. *Worship Old and New.* (Grand Rapids: Zondervan, 1982).

NOTES

1 Thomas C. Oden, *Pastoral Theology: Essentials of Ministry*, San Francisco: Harper & Row, 1983, p. 88.

2 *Worship: recovering a spiritual dynamic for renewal*, GRID, World Vision of Australia, Box 339c, Melbourne 3001, Australia.

3 Don Wardlaw, 'A two-track program of educating a congregation in worship,' unpublished paper.

4 Don Wardlaw, 'Letting the whole person worship,' unpublished paper, p. 3.

Photo: New Times

21

Listen to the prophets

(Material in chapters 21–34 can be enriched by viewing video tape four.)

The ministry of prophets was very important in New Testament times. Paul regarded it highly, urging the Corinthians to seek this important spiritual gift (1 Corinthians 14:1, 39). Paul wanted them all to speak in tongues, but even more to prophesy. Why? Because tongues helps the individual; prophecy helps the church. In the three lists of church ministries (Romans 12, 1 Corinthians 12 and Ephesians 4), only one ministry is mentioned in all of them — the prophetic.

Prophecy is a direct communication from God for a particular people at a particular time and place, for a particular purpose. The Divine Word also comes through Jesus, through Scripture, through circumstances, and through visions (more commonly in non-Western cultures). The Lord wants to continue speaking to his people, he is longing to communicate directly with us; the problem is there aren't enough people willing to pay the price of being his mouthpiece. In the Bible, 'generally speaking the Lord is generally speaking'.

Prophecy is not the same as preaching or teaching, although there may often be some overlap (e.g. some prophecy, as in Acts 13:16f. sounds like sermonic teaching); effective preaching may at times be prophetic, at least in part. 'Prophecy is distinguished from teaching by its character of a direct message in relation to the situation ... and by its reference to a particular divine revelation.'[1] In 1 Corinthians 12:28, the prophet is distinguished from the teacher, and in Ephesians 4:11 from the evangelist.

The teacher bases his message on the given tradition, while the prophet speaks on the basis of a personal revelation. The prophet speaks under the immediate control of the Holy Spirit: the prophet's message is not the result of reflection, reasoning or feeling. 'False prophets' speak from their own heart, the true prophet out of the mouth of the Lord (Jeremiah 23:16).

Prophecy gives the church fresh insights into God's truth (Ephesians 3), of guidance about the future (as in this story in Acts 11),[2] or encouragement (1 Corinthians 14:3; 1 Timothy 1:18), or inspiration or correction. It either edifies the church or brings it under judgment ('God is in this place!' — see 1 Corinthians 14:25).

The biblical prophets combined judgment with hope. Their messages were sometimes very challenging: prophets 'disturb the comfortable' while pastors 'comfort the disturbed'! Prophets 'tell it like it is'. Paul told the Thessalonians not to despise prophesyings ('inspired messages', 1 Thessalonians 5:20–22) but 'put all things to the test: keep what is good and avoid every kind of evil'. We can be sure that God still wants to speak to his people by this means; we can also be sure that there will be 'false prophets' today as there were throughout biblical times.

The Lord is sowing good seed, the devil evil weeds (Matthew 13:24–30). Sometimes, in various sects, 'prophetic utterances' have been given a higher status than Scripture itself. However, although the devil might be at work, this shouldn't hinder our being open to the Word of the Lord. We must 'censor' prophets (the prophets at Antioch came from Jerusalem, and no doubt Barnabas knew they were 'credentialled' by the church there), discipline them, correct them.

The gift of 'discernment of spirits' is given to the church — then and now — to help sort out true from false prophets. Here's a practical way to 'judge' present-day prophets: if someone in the church believes he or she has a message from the Lord, that person ought to submit it first to the pastors/elders, so that it comes under the authority of the church leaders. Perhaps this could be done in writing.

At this point, we ought to ask the general question, How do we test spiritual gifts to see if they indeed are from God? David Watson offers these seven guidelines: Is Jesus Lord of that person's life? Is Jesus acknowledged as perfect man and perfect God? Is the manifestation of the gift in accordance with the Scriptures? Is there true holiness and godliness about that person? Is there submission to church leaders? Is the church edified through this gift? Is love the controlling factor?[3]

Let us encourage one another to listen more carefully to the Lord. Ours is a very noisy age, and silence is needed if we are to hear God's 'still small voice' again. A final word from Hans Kung. A church in which the prophets are not heard 'declines and becomes a spiritless organisation; outwardly everything may seem all right, things run smoothly, according to plan and along ordered paths ... but inwardly it will be a place where the Spirit can no longer blow when and where he wills'.[4]

Discuss: How would your congregation cope with a few prophets in their midst? What safeguards would you put in place to guard against 'false prophets'? How can your worship services be more open to a 'word from the Lord' coming from someone other than the preacher? Some larger Pentecostal churches with very effective evangelistic services are now excluding tongues and prophecy from services oriented towards outsiders. Any comment on that trend?

Further Reading: David Watson. *I Believe in the Church.* London: Hodder and Stoughton, 1978. The article 'Prophecy, Prophet' in Walter A. Elwell, (ed.), *Evangelical Dictionary of Theology.* Grand Rapids: Baker Book House, 1984.

NOTES

1 David Watson, *I Believe in the Church*, London: Hodder & Stoughton, 1978, p. 258, quoting from J-J von Allman (ed.), *Vocabulary of the Bible*, Lutterworth, p. 348.

2 In the apostolic church, there are several instances of foretelling (Acts 11:27f, 21:9ff, Paul in 1 Corinthians 15:51, 1 Thessalonians 4:14-18, Peter in 2 Peter 3:10ff., and of course the Book of Revelation).

3 David Watson, *I Believe in the Church*, London: Hodder & Stoughton, 1978, pp. 112-3.

4 Hans Kung, *The Church*, London: Burns and Oates, 1968, p. 433.

22

Compassion and mercy

These believers were concerned not only about 'saving souls' — evangelism — but helping others deprived of necessary daily needs. Unfortunately Christians have sometimes emphasised one or the other of these two areas of essential ministry, rather than both: creating 'an unbiblical divorce between the kerygma and the diakonia'.[1] Jim Wallis put it well: 'The greatest need in our time is not simply for kerygma, the preaching of the gospel, nor for diakonia, service on behalf of justice, nor for charisma, the experience of the Spirit's gifts, nor even for propheteia, the challenging of the king. The greatest need of our time is for koinonia, the call to simply be the church — to love one another, and to offer our life for the sake of the world'.[2]

A theological understanding of Christian social concern begins with the character of God. He is a 'social God',[3] relating within the community of the Trinity, and, in the Incarnation of Jesus Christ, with his creatures on this planet. Jesus came with a mandate to preach, liberate and heal (Luke 4:18-19) and commissions his followers to do the same as he did (John 20:21).

So the church, the body of Christ, does in its world what Jesus did in his: no more, no less. It adopts Jesus' stance towards others: that of a servant. And it will be called to account at the Great Judgment relative to the presence or absence of ministries of compassion to the poor (Matthew 25:31–46).

Who are the poor? They are people who have no 'place'. The materially poor are deprived of a place within the bounty of the community; the lonely, the imprisoned, or the emotionally poor do not have a place within a loving family or community; the politically poor do not have a place in the decision-making processes of their government; refugees are 'displaced', without a part of the earth to call their own; the spiritually deprived do not have a place in the kingdom.

Our Christian compassion must address all these issues. The meaning of Christian 'hospitality' is simply our opening up our hearts, our lives, our homes, our communities, to the 'wretched of the earth'. Hospitality is providing a place for Jesus, who is still poor today. I asked some very poor rural Brazilians what made them anxious or fearful. A sad-looking mother said, 'I cannot warm my children with just one blanket'. A man who had the face and hands of half a century's hard labour said, 'I toil and toil but have very little to show for it'. I was very moved. What do I say to them? Maybe my tears spoke louder than any words. I felt helpless, but I also felt a solidarity with them in their despair.

'Compassion' comes from the Latin *pati* and *cum* — 'to suffer with'. The church takes Jesus as its model for compassion. Twelve times in the gospels, Jesus or his Father — God — are said to be 'moved with compassion' for worried and helpless people (e.g. Matthew 9:36). Our Lord sends us his followers into the world to 'be compassionate as your Father is compassionate' (Luke 6:36). How does compassion work? In the same way God's does: he sends Jesus into the world to be with us. He emptied himself and became a servant (Philippians 2). That gives us dignity: we must be worth a lot if he is willing to be our slave! He says to us: 'I will be with you always until the end of the age' (Matthew 28:20). We are not alone.

So compassion is more than sympathy — 'feeling sorry' for the poor. It's not 'pity' for someone weak or inferior. Compassion is a 'doing verb' — relieving the pain of others, not just emoting about it. But it's more than 'helping the less fortunate' — that's elitist and paternalistic. Compassion, says Matthew Fox, is the world's richest energy source.[4]

A few days before his death, Rabbi Heschel said, 'There is an old idea in Judaism that God suffers when we suffer ... Even when a criminal is hanged on the gallows, God cries. God identifies himself with the misery on this earth. I can help God by reducing human suffering, human anguish and human misery'.[5]

But there's so much pain — where do I start? In the Matthew text describing Jesus' compassion (9:35-38), our Lord then turns to his disciples and says 'There's so much to do, and so few to do it,

PRAY!' The first thing to do is to pray! Prayer tunes us in to the heart of God. Prayer helps us focus on others and their needs. Prayer turns frustration and anger into hope. A by-product of prayer is peace, without which we will never act appropriately in an unjust world.

I believe it is important for every wage or salary earner, with their family or community, to give a proportion away regularly to the poor — in one's own country and overseas. You could sponsor a child, or give directly to projects among the poor (more of your dollar gets there that way). Choose an organisation, preferably, that is committed to a 'need not creed' approach (as Jesus was, rather than giving to your kind of people only). Or you can give through your own denomination; whatever you do, try to be well informed about the situations you are supporting.

Discuss: (1) Who is 'hurting' in some way in your neighbourhood? (2) What community resources or groups exist to meet these needs? (3) What unmet needs exist which your church could organise to meet? (4) It is possible to assist with aid and development many more of the overseas poor, if we and our governments had a will to do so. One of the tragedies of our time is Christians who 'walk by on the other side of the sea'. What percentage of your church's families give regularly to a Christian aid organisation? What could your church do to encourage more to be involved in world-wide ministries of mercy?

Bible Study: Romans 15:17–29. First look at Galatians 2:6–10: why would Paul need this reminder, do you think? What can you do, above what is done by government agencies for the poor in our country? 'Every Christian wage-earner and his/her family or community should give regularly to the poor overseas.' Agree? Many churches take up an extra offering once a month (at a communion service) for the poor; discuss the possibility of this idea in your church. How should this money be dispersed?

A Prayer: Bob Pierce, the founder of World Vision, prayed that his heart would be broken for the things that break the heart of God. Perhaps you and I could pray like this: 'Lord, the needs of the world are so great; evil and pain are everywhere; I can't do everything, I can't do much, but I can do something. It would be a privilege, Lord, to share the pain of others, and so to alleviate some of your pain. I pray through Jesus Christ my Lord, who suffered so much pain for me. Amen.'

Further Reading: Matthew Fox. *A Spirituality Named Compassion.* San Francisco: Harper & Row, 1979; Donald McNeill. Douglas A. Morrison, Henri J. M. Nouwen. *Compassion: A Reflection on the Christian Life.* New York: Doubleday, 1983.

NOTES

1 C. Rene Padilla (ed.), *The New Face of Evangelicalism*, London: Hodder & Stoughton, 1976.
2 Jim Wallis, *Sojourners* 9:1, January 1980, p. 11.
3 Kenneth Leech, *The Social God*, London: Sheldon, 1981.
4 Matthew Fox, *A Spirituality Named Compassion*, San Francisco, Harper & Row, 1979, p. [i].
5 Cited by Fox, ibid, p. 19.

23

Financial generosity

Money is a sensitive subject. The 'hip-pocket nerve' is a tender part of our being. The Bible has more to say about the use or misuse of money than about either heaven or hell! Jesus spoke more about money than any other single subject. In the Sermon on the Mount, he says where our treasure is, there will our hearts be also. In most of his letters, Paul refers directly or more subtly to our responsibilities to share in the costs of ministry or the needs of the poor. Jacques Ellul suggests money is one of the 'spiritual forces' with which we struggle (Ephesians 6:12).[1]

It's the only impersonal thing to which Jesus gave a proper name — Mammon. Jesus thought of money in some sort of spiritual sense, competing with God for our allegiance. The only way to break the power of Mammon is to give money away. Money is a root of many evils: for televangelists with their millions or you and me with our thousands or hundreds! Your chequebook stubs are a pretty good indicator of the kind of person you are! Each of the 'disciples' gave as much as possible towards this relief effort (Acts 11:29).

A church that's alive is a generous church; a 'penny-pinching' attitude is a mark of a church that's dying. As I type the phone has just rung. I've been raising money to send Bibles to Russian pastors and church leaders. The call went like this (we'll call him Frank): 'Rowland, how much was that appeal target?' '$62,500.'

'How much have you got?' 'Well, it's early yet but $15,000 has come in.' Frank: 'I'd like to make up the balance: I'll give $50,000'!

In most churches there are millions of dollars lying around in assets and savings: let's use them for the kingdom! Today the average Western family has more than fifty per cent of its income available for what would have been regarded as 'non-essentials' by our grandparents; in 1900 it was four per cent. Money is important for the church, but the church does not exist to raise money. It's a pity that many churches are often seen by the community-at-large to be preoccupied with fund-raising. The public exposures they have are geared most often towards this end.

One survey among a group of 'nominal' church people found that most believed the pastor's main job was balancing the church's budget! (Surveys among pastors show them to be generous givers, but they rate the financial management of the church low on their list of professional priorities.) We came into the world with nothing, and we shall leave the same way. In the meantime we have a responsibility to manage the resources entrusted to us by God. Freely we have received, so freely we give (Matthew 10:8).

'Stewardship' is everything we do with everything we have. Stewardship begins with the idea that God owns all things — so we're not giving to God what is ours, but releasing what is already his. Stewardship is ministry. (So 'if God ever gives anything to you, get rid of it quickly' said one person who realised he became covetous for more if he hung on to it too long.) A steward (e.g. a banker) manages someone else's money or property (Luke 16:1). Christian stewardship is all about responsibility, loyalty and commitment — being trustworthy (2 Corinthians 4:2) rather than merely raising money.

For many churches a 'stewardship campaign' has a sting in its tail. 'Stewardship' is like the word 'blue' said one church leader — 'blue' moods, 'blue' movies, etc. A good word, but bad associations. Stewardship campaigns in 'dead' churches remind me of giving a box of tissues to a pneumonia sufferer: it may be of some comfort, but is irrelevant to the victim's recovery which depends on other factors.

But that said, let us be as forthright about money as the Bible is. Tithing — the Lord's tax for the use of the earth, because it's his — is a fundamental requirement for all of us. That doesn't mean we're to be legalistic about tithing. The motivation should come from love not law (Romans 13:10), but a tenth of net income given away to others is a good place to start. Jesus endorsed tithing, but said we have to do much more — practise justice, mercy and faithfulness (Matthew 23:23, Luke 11:42). We don't tithe to be 'blessed', although we will be; nor to avoid God's curse, though the Bible is up-front about that too (we have no option to give or not to give, 1 Samuel 8, Malachi 3:8–10); nor to secure our salvation (remember John Tetzel, who even promised pardon for 'the sins you intend to commit' if one bought his indulgences?).

Gifts above the tenth are 'freewill offerings' (Deuteronomy 16:10–11, Exodus 36:7, Leviticus 22:21), 'festival tithes' (Deuteronomy 14:22–27, 16:3,13,16) and 'charity tithes' (levied every third year for the poor, Deuteronomy 14:28–29, 26:12–15). The givers in the gospels who receive Jesus' commendation are not mere tithers, but people like Mary who gave her precious gift, Zaccheus who gave half his goods, and the widow who gave everything. A pastor's sermon on tithing was titled 'The Sermon on the Amount'! This subject is so much a cause of dissension in churches we ought now to face some practical issues.

How to raise more money for your church.

Here are some principles:

- Churches where people have truly 'first given themselves to the Lord' (2 Corinthians 8:5) are more likely to meet their financial commitments. Ultimately the truest gift is the gift of self. When our hearts are right with God, generosity follows. In the familiar words of Isaac Watts, love so amazing, so divine, demands my soul, my life, my all.
- You only truly keep what you give away (Proverbs 11:24, 25).
- God's work done in God's way will not lack God's supply. However, we are God's ears, eyes, hands. Those in need, or in Christian service ministries ought not to be reduced to 'beggary': that's demeaning, and dishonouring to God.
- If people feel the church has truly been meaningful in their lives, they'll want to give generously.
- The more visionary a church is, with meaningful programs to involve people enthusiastically, the less trouble that church will have raising funds. The church with very few significant activities between Sundays has a big problem! So has the church that tries to get money out of people for programs which someone else has decided is good for them!
- People ought to give thoughtfully — to people and programs, not because there's a fund-raising effort — and faithfully (1 Corinthians 4:2).
- Committed people give regularly and proportionately (1 Corinthians 16:2). However, for any special project there will be some who will give very generously.

- People mostly give because other people they trust ask them to, and give most and most frequently when asked face to face.
- While there may be nothing wrong with 'stewardship campaigns' as such, the need for them is in many cases a sign of the church's lack of on-going commitment. The church should not need to 'drum up business' for its general budget this way. However, a 'faith-promise' scheme has proved effective in many evangelical churches for special missionary giving: the vast majority of these churches then find their 'home-base' needs are more than met anyway when our sights are lifted to God's world-wide mission.
- If raising money for a special program or event, devise a schedule that runs backwards from the completion date, setting deadlines to reach each step at a prescribed time. Set some realistic goals; a time-frame that won't get people suffering from 'donor-fatigue'; and appoint one worker (previous large givers are often the best) for every ten prospects.
- Matthew 10:9-15 suggests that mission enterprises ought quickly to become indigenous: the worker supported by those he or she serves (see also 1 Timothy 5:17). We give 'seed money' then the young church or enterprise takes over. Giving too much for too long is paternalistic: many younger churches throughout the two-thirds world have not been taught to be self-reliant. So new Christians everywhere should be taught the necessity of regular, proportional giving.

The finance board

Churches above 200 people need a small (3 or 5 person) committee to handle financial matters. (Churches of any size ought never allow just one person to count offerings or keep the books: this allows too much room for temptation.) Above 1000, make it 7 people. This board ought to be accountable to the governing body of the church, and should be composed of people who are either accountants or visionaries, with the balance (maybe the chairperson) loaded slightly in favour of the second group! Accountants are people whose financial foot is near the brake; entrepreneurs have theirs on the accelerator.

Each group needs the other. Accountants hold us accountable for the budgetary decisions we have made, but they sometimes don't have the gift of faith: that's OK, so long as you don't allow them to dominate areas of decision-making requiring faith! They help us to be realistic, but when all the facts are in, the extra 'plus' of faith will help move mountains such as 'but we can't afford it', 'we'll never make it', etc.

The finance board should know how the weekly offerings break down: how many give what amount with what regularity? It is not necessary for anyone to know who gives how much (although some churches and denominations have systems which reveal this information).

Guidance for church treasurers

Most denominations have a system for guiding local church treasurers, and systems vary. However, here's a check-list:
- Always present finance reports that a child of 13 with normal intelligence can understand!
- Church budgets should be realistic but with a touch of optimism; present the budget to the church with last year's income and expenditure.
- Prepare a cash-flow/liquidity plan to prevent large amounts lying idle: short-term overnight investments can earn interest.
- Make sure your record systems (day book, columnar cash books, petty cash etc.) are simple — and a few people should know them well.
- Insurances OK?
- The pastor should be paid, even if the church has to go into overdraft to do it (though that situation should not go on for too long).

The idea of a church bank

At Blackburn Baptist Church, we figured people had millions of dollars tied up in their real estate or savings which could be used for ministry. So we started a church bank, invited people to lend any amount for any length of time, nominate the rate of interest (up to State Savings Bank interest — many lent money interest-free). It worked on a pass-book system: they could draw out any amount up to $5000 at call, or larger amounts with 7 days' notice.

The finance board of the church figured how much of the total should be readily available in liquid funds, how much invested at higher interest in a carefully balanced investment portfolio, and how much released for various projects. We had access to more than $300,000 through this means. But be careful it's managed properly, and within the law!

Lifestyle

I have wept in the night
For the shortness of sight
That to somebody's need made me blind;
But I never have yet
Felt a tinge of regret
For being a little too kind. (Anonymous)

We make a living by what we get; we make a life by what we give. But humans, because of their insecurity, tend to be covetous, acquisitive. The desire to possess is very strong, and the more we have the more we want. Deficits, inflation, cutting down forests, the greenhouse effect, the destruction of the ozonosphere — all are caused by greed. It's interesting that Christians who take a lot of the Bible literally don't do that with our Lord's words to the rich young ruler: 'Go, sell all you have and give the money to the poor ...' (Mark 10:21). (Our reading: 'Keep most of what you have but be nice!').

The Bible is clear that we should provide for our family's necessities (1 Timothy 5:8), and each person and family/community ought to figure out where the threshold is between needs and wants. It's good to have what money can buy, but most important to have what money cannot buy.

- Give up shopping as a form of recreation. If you don't really need it, don't buy it! Get by with less. Our grandparents had the slogan 'Use it up. Wear it out. Make it do. Do without'.
- Fast foods are very expensive in relation to their nutritional value.
- Some find the graduated tithe a good way to extend their giving: you start by budgeting for the basic necessities, give ten per cent of that, then fifteen per cent of the next, say, $5000 you earn, twenty per cent of the next $5000, and so on.[2]

Bible Study: 2 Corinthians 8:1-15. Look at verses 8 and 10. Why 'advice' rather than a 'commandment'? (see chapter 9:7–12). The only obligation they are put under is the Lordship of Christ. Why? Is it true that the poor are generally more faithful givers than the rich? What is the point of the reference to Jesus (8:9)? Can you figure out how verse 15 can apply to your church?

Further Reading: Richard Foster. *Money, Sex and Power.* San Francisco: Harper & Row, 1987; Tom Sine. *The Mustard Seed Conspiracy.* Waco: Word Books, 1981. Ask your denominational headquarters for their manual for church treasurers.

NOTES

1 Jacques Ellul, *Money and Power*, Downers Grove, Ill.: Intervarsity Press, 1984.
2 Ronald Sider, *Rich Christians in an Age of Hunger*, Downers Grove, Ill.: InterVarsity Press, 1977.

Photo: Eddy Marmur

24

Who's in charge?

Elders or 'presbyters' appear very early as leaders in the church along with apostles, prophets and teachers. Probably the Jerusalem church's rule, where James had a prominent role, was modelled after that of the synagogue (Acts 11:30, 21:18). But these leaders felt they had some responsibility for the church-at-large as well (Acts 15:2, 6, 23; 16:4).

Paul and Barnabas had elders appointed in the churches they founded on their first missionary journey (Acts 14:23). The New Testament also mentions bishops (*episkopoi*): in Acts 20:17-28 and Titus 1:5-7 the two terms seem interchangeable. However it's interesting that the distinction between elder and bishop first became marked at Antioch, where Ignatius became sole bishop (the historians call it 'monarchical episcopate') early in the second century A.D. Apparently by this time many churches had a bishop, assisted by presbyters and deacons: a three-fold order of 'set apart' ministry.

Which raises the interesting question: how were churches supposed to be governed in New Testament times; and how should they be organised today? There have been three broad answers to these questions: the episcopal model (rule by bishops); presbyterianism (rule by elders) and congregationalism (a supposedly more 'democratic' system, where each local congregation governs its own affairs).

Notice that the church in Antioch did not consult anyone else when Paul was added to their staff, nor when Barnabas and Paul went forth as missionaries. By then, five people were named as leaders in that church (Acts 13:1). Further, when Barnabas and Paul set up churches, they appointed elders, and urged local pastors like Titus to do the same (Titus 1:5) — a task a modern 'bishop' would have the power to do. So, in brief, the answer to the church government question is: there wasn't a timeless blue-print given to the early church; indeed combinations of all three models are probably necessary and wise in the church today. Leon Morris says, wisely:

> A consideration of the evidence leaves us with the conclusion that it is impossible to read back any of our modern systems into the apostolic age. If we are determined to shut our eyes to all that conflicts with our own system we may find it there, but scarcely otherwise. It is better to recognise that in the New Testament church there were elements that were capable of being developed into the episcopal, presbyterian, and congregational systems and which in point of fact have so developed. But while there is no reason that any modern Christian should not hold fast to a particular church polity and rejoice in its values, that does not give one licence to unchurch others whose reading of the evidence is different.[1]

Decision-making processes

Once the Holy Spirit had communicated this move to the church, and they had prayed about the matter, the decision to go ahead was made without fuss. In a church that's alive there may not be an absence of disagreement, or even of conflict, but issues are settled amicably. Probably the leaders and church at Antioch agreed unanimously to this missionary idea. Unanimity is nice, and should be sought wherever possible. But in a 'fallen world' sometimes the legalistic quest for unanimity can lead to 'rule by the crank'. One person can be the odd-person-out, and can hold up the whole process if allowed to. Now that doesn't mean that occasionally this one person may not be right, but that's generally the exception.

Decision-making has cultural overtones. In a tribal setting where the life of the group is vested in one individual leader, he (or she) may decide for the group, and the rest are willing to go along. In an 'oligarchy' a small group decides. In a democracy, everyone wants a say. Sometimes the last two modes are combined, where a congregation vests in a small group the power to make certain decisions between members' meetings.

All these three general methods of 'government' are appropriate in different cultural settings. Probably we should search for a combination of all three: with the necessary checks and balances to ensure that individuals and small groups don't accrue to themselves too much power. In the long run, the acid test is whether the whole church 'owns' the decisions made.

Discuss: (1) Get someone to research your denomination's history in the area of 'church government'. To what extent has your church inherited a model which is no longer appropriate? What changes would you suggest? (2) Discuss frankly the issue of 'power' in your church. Who or what group wields power, with what outcomes?

Further Reading: Ray S. Anderson. *Minding God's Business.* Grand Rapids: Eerdmans, 1986; James D. Anderson and Ezra Earl Jones. *The Management of Ministry.* San Francisco: Harper & Row, 1978; C. Peter Wagner. *Leading Your Church to Growth.* Ventura: Regal, 1984; Edward Schillebeeckx. *The Church with a Human Face.* London: SCM, 1985; Lyle Schaller. *Effective Church Planning.* Nashville: Abingdon, 1979; Lyle Schaller. *Looking in the Mirror: Self-Appraisal in the Local Church.* Nashville: Abingdon, 1985.

NOTES

1 Leon Morris, 'Church Government' in Walter A. Elwell (ed.), *Evangelical Dictionary of Theology*, Michigan: Baker Book House, 1984, pp. 238ff. Morris made the same point in his *Ministers of God*, London: IVF, 1964.

25

Do your people know their spiritual gifts?

There were five 'prophets and teachers' in the Antioch church. Who are the 'prophets and teachers' in your church? Do people know their 'spiritual gifts' in your church? Do you know why you're on the earth and not yet in heaven? If there's one key indicator separating fruitful from sterile churches it is the degree to which ordinary members of the church know their spiritual gifts and are encouraged to minister according to these 'charisms'.

The word Paul likes to use is *charisma* (plural, *charismata*) from *charis*, grace. You can read about these 'grace–gifts' in Romans 12:6–8, 1 Corinthians 12:4–11, 28–30; Ephesians 4:7–12. The following statements summarise very briefly what is important about spiritual gifts: (1) The gift (person) of the Holy Spirit is received when one becomes a Christian. (2) The gifts of the Spirit are special abilities every Christian receives to edify the church. (3) Natural talents are given at birth (or conception), spiritual gifts as a result of new birth: some amazing spiritual gifts operate through ordinarily-talented people sometimes; conversely, a multitalented person isn't necessarily a mature Christian (so be careful in selecting people for office in the church). (4) Spiritual gifts may be either miraculous or non-miraculous. (5) The operation of spiritual gifts in the church should promote unity and love: their use has to be monitored by the church's leadership to ensure these ends. (6) We must avoid two extremes — 'charisphobia' (avoidance of certain gifts on the basis of their miraculous or inexplicable nature), and 'charismania' (a fascination with or concentration on the miraculous gifts). (7) 'The Spirit bestows his charismata for the edification of the church, the formation of Christian character, and the service of the community. The reception of a spiritual gift [brings] serious responsibility; [it is] essentially an opportunity for self-giving in sacrificial service for others.'[1]

God our Father delights in giving gifts (Luke 11:9-13). He encourages us to ask, in Jesus' name (that is, for the glory of Jesus). 'Lord, bless me', you may ask. The Father replies: 'What specific blessing do you want?' 'Lord, give me a gift of love.' 'For whom?' 'Lord, I need power.' 'What sort of power, to do what?' Be specific! However, note that the Spirit is sovereign: we may ask, but he gives what is best for us and for others through us. So we should willingly receive whatever he gives us. Our attitude should be one of expectancy, availability and humility (1 Corinthians 12:11).

The English evangelist David Watson used to say 'The Holy Spirit is a gentleman!' He doesn't violate human personality. He gives gifts to the church so that Christ will be glorified, and the body of Christ become strong. There are varieties of gifts, so that the body, the church, can function properly. These gifts are not given to some and not others: all may be recipients of the Lord's largesse. When a gift is given, it is not 'my' gift: it is the Spirit's gift, to the church, through me as a channel.

One of the beautiful things about a church open to all the spiritual gifts is the complementarity of ministries that result. Some gifts are private, some for public use; some are miraculous, others what we might call 'ordinary'. The dispensing of spiritual gifts should not produce feelings of superiority or inferiority: we do not need churches full of people with speaking or musical gifts, for example!

Finally a warning: Do some spiritual gifts split churches? No, the Holy Spirit is not destructive. People wanting to exercise improper power split churches. The presence or absence of a spiritual gift may be the occasion, never the cause of such dissension! Here are six guidelines for your church in this area: (1) Follow the guidance of Scripture. All the gifts are available to all the church for all time, but there are clear biblical rules for order in their public use (see 1 Corinthians 12-14). (2) Work hard to produce a loving church. Be willing to allow some to make mistakes. But, you ask, 'Isn't that dangerous sometimes?' Yes, but a 'dangerous' church is better than a dead one! (3) All spiritual gifts are expressions of the compassion of Christ; they are not given for some to display their superior spirituality. (4) Gifts are for sharing (e.g. 1 Corinthians 14:26). (5) Encourage those who are a little tentative about exercising their spiritual gift. (6) Pray especially for gifts that will strengthen the church in love.

Exercise: Buy copies of Robert Hillman's *27 Spiritual Gifts* (Melbourne: JBCE, 1986) and try some of the Bible studies on pp. 134ff.

Further Reading: Robert Hillman. *27 Spiritual Gifts*. Melbourne: JBCE, 1986; David Watson. *One in the Spirit.* London: Hodder & Stoughton, 1975; Charles E. Hummel. *Fire in the Fireplace: Contemporary Charismatic Renewal.* Illinois: Intervarsity Press, 1978; David Watson. *I Believe in the Church.* London: Hodder & Stoughton, 1978; Michael Cassidy. *Bursting the Wineskins.* London: Hodder & Stoughton, 1983; Donald Bridge and David Phypers. *Spiritual Gifts and the Church.* London: IVP, 1973; George Mallone. *Those Controversial Gifts.* London: Hodder & Stoughton, 1983; David Pawson. *The Normal Christian Birth.* London: Hodder & Stoughton, 1989.

NOTES

1 J. G. S. S.. Thomson and W. A.. Elwell, 'Spiritual Gifts' in Walter A. Elwell (ed.), *Evangelical Dictionary of Theology*, Michigan: Baker Book House, 1984, pp. 1042ff.

26

Affirming diversity

Note the varied backgrounds from which the Antioch church's leadership came (Acts 13:1). Barnabas was a Cypriot Jew; Simeon ('the Black') probably came from Africa; Lucius (probably not the same person as Acts' author) came from Cyrene in North Africa; Manaen was brought up in aristocratic circles; and Paul was an ex-Pharisee and trained rabbi. Such a diverse group willingly fellowshipping together would have been rare in the Mediterranean world.

In 1977 British New Testament scholar James Dunn wrote a book entitled *Unity and Diversity in the New Testament* where in 470 well argued pages he concludes that there's a marked degree of diversity within the first century church; there are many different expressions of the faith within the New Testament; there was no single normative form of Christianity in the first century. Their only unifying factor, he says, was their allegiance to Jesus.[1]

Similarly, Oxford professor John Macquarrie, in his *Christian Unity and Christian Diversity*, offers the thesis that diversity is just as essential as unity to the well-being of the Christian church. 'To combine unity with freedom is a very difficult task, and the temptations to uniformity are very great ... A stark unity freezes the church and inhibits development. A sheer diversity would dissipate the church and cause her to disappear. Only unity and diversity together can be fruitful.'[2] He borrows an expression from

Don Cupitt, 'One Jesus, many Christs'.... 'Jesus has been seen as moralist, prophet, apocalyptist, hero, redeemer, priest, and king'.[3] Oliver Wendell Holmes once said he wouldn't give a fig for the simplicity this side of complexity, but he would give his life for the simplicity on the other side of complexity. All heresy, G. K. Chesterton affirms somewhere, is a narrowing down unduly of what is essentially a complex reality. Each part of the church needs the other parts.

What binds us together is not the 'purity' of our doctrinal viewpoint, nor the way we worship and serve the Lord ('orthodoxy' and 'orthopraxis'), but our common allegiance to Jesus as Lord, and our being children of the same Father, united by the same Spirit. The church ought never to be a universal 'sausage machine', turning out clones of one sort or another.

Discuss: Who is 'different' in your church or community? Is your church fellowship open to people of differing socio-economic, theological, or ethnic backgrounds?

Further Reading: James D. G.. Dunn. *Unity and Diversity in the New Testament: An Inquiry into the Character of Earliest Christianity.* London: SCM, 1977; John Macquarrie. *Christian Unity and Christian Diversity.* Philadelphia: SCM, 1975.

NOTES

1 James D. G. Dunn, *Unity and Diversity in the New Testament: An Inquiry into the Character of Earliest Christianity*, London: SCM, 1977.

2 John Macquarrie, *Christian Unity and Christian Diversity*, Philadelphia: SCM, 1975, preface, p. 7.

3 Don Cupitt, 'One Jesus, Many Christs?', in S. W. Sykes and J. P. Clayton, (eds.), *Christ, Faith and History*, Cambridge: CUP 1972, pp. 131–44.

27

Social justice: get involved!

Paul says that when we are united in Christ Jesus the barriers between races, slaves/freepersons and sexes are removed (Galatians 3:28).

A Christian can no longer pray the words of the Jewish daily thanksgiving, 'I thank thee, O Lord, that thou hast not made me a Gentile, a slave or a woman'. This principle — that we are all united in Christ, and that racist, economic, and sexist divisions have been obliterated — has taken a while to catch on in the church. But these Christians at Antioch had certainly triumphed in the area of racism. It took another eighteen centuries to come around to abolishing slavery; and we're working on the problems of sexism in this century.

Actually, we're still struggling with the other two as well: the 11 a.m. worship time in the U.S. has been called the most segregated hour in the nation's week, and the Dutch Reformed Church in South Africa is very reluctantly dismantling its institutionalised racism. (I met an intelligent white Pentecostal Christian in South Africa who told me he believed blacks were created by God to serve whites!) In the area of economics, white western Christians are among the wealthiest people in the world. They are potentially the most powerful lobby in the world: but they don't lobby governments in the area of wealth redistribution. In Australia, the most effective recent lobbying efforts have been about issues of self-interest: a proposed 'bill of rights', consumption tax, and a fringe-benefits tax, at a time when we have record stockpiles of unsold grain, and are giving less of it away than at any time for twenty-five years!

Justice is all — and only — about the uses of power. Injustice is the mis-use, non-use or abuse of power. In the Bible justice is personal (living a righteous, just life), forensic (relating to matters of law), and social (our treatment of the poor). The Bible is full of God's concern for justice, from his holding Cain accountable for the murder of his brother in Genesis, to a similar accountability by the secular powers persecuting Christians, described in the graphic imagery of the Book of Revelation. When Micah summarises the essence of what it means to worship the Lord, he says it is doing justice, loving kindness, and living in humble fellowship with our God (Micah 6:8).

Jesus similarly sums up 'the really important teachings of the law' — 'justice and mercy and honesty' (Matthew 23:23).[1] Elsewhere Jesus gives us 'the great commandment ... love the Lord your God with all your heart, with all your soul, and with all your mind and with all your strength ... [and] love your neighbour as you love yourself' (Mark 12:30–31). It is interesting that evangelical Christians rarely agree with Micah or Jesus when asked to highlight what are for them the most important doctrines: outside of the Wesleyan, some Catholic, and a few conciliar churches' creeds or statements of faith, I can find no evangelical 'doctrinal basis' before the Lausanne Congress (1974) that explicitly mentions justice or love!

A church that is alive is concerned with much more than persons 'making decisions for Christ'. Mission for them is not restricted to compassion for the lost, but also for those suffering pain and injustice.

Discuss: (1) Why are white, Western middle class Christians loath to get involved in 'justice' issues? Why was justice important for Jesus but not so much for us? (2) Share your reactions to this statement: 'The Bible was written by the poor for the poor. So the rich — that's us — will be severely handicapped in really understanding the Bible'.

Further Reading: Donal Dorr. *Spirituality and Justice.* New York: Orbis, 1984; Reinhold Niebuhr. *Moral Man and Immoral Society.* New York: Scribner's, 1932/1960; Rosino Gibellini. *The Liberation Theology Debate.* London: SCM, 1987; Peter Philp. *Journey with the Poor.* Blackburn, Victoria: Collins Dove, 1988; Justo L. Gonzalez and Catherine G. Gonzalez. *Liberation Preaching: The Pulpit and the Oppressed.* Nashville: Abingdon, 1980; Dominique LaPierre. *The City of Joy.* London: Arrow Books, 1986; Walter Brueggemann. *The Prophetic Imagination.* Philadelphia: Fortress Press, 1985; Waldron Scott. *Bring Forth Justice.* London: Eerdmans, 1980; Walter Wink. *The Powers*, vol 1: *Naming the Powers*, vol. 2: *Unmasking the Powers.* Philadelphia: Fortress Press, 1984, 1986.

NOTES

1 Donal Dorr's *Spirituality and Justice*, New York: Orbis, 1984, posits the thesis, based on Micah's affirmation and Jesus' paraphrase of it, that all Christians need three conversions: political, social and personal.

28

Worship: who's the audience?

'Whoever offers praise glorifies me!' says the Lord (Psalm 50:23). Worship and praise are the ceaseless, joyous occupation of heaven. The angels, seraphs and cherubim cry, 'Holy, holy, holy is the Lord of hosts ... You are worthy, O Lord, to receive glory and honour and power'. In worship we are not asking God to give himself to us so much as giving ourselves to him. And the wonder of it all is that the Almighty, Immortal, Invisible God will accept our adoration and praise and thanksgiving. The God who needs nothing delights to receive our adoration. What incredible grace!

We have already said some things about worship (chapter 20). Here we take this foundational subject a little further. The Christians at Antioch were 'serving the Lord' and fasting when the Holy Spirit spoke to them (Acts 13:2). 'Serving the Lord' is worship; worship is serving the Lord — it is nothing else. So phrases like 'Worship Service' or 'Service of Worship' are tautologies. To worship God is to serve him.[1]

Worship, for a Christian, is everything we do for the glory of God (Romans 12:1, 2; 1 Corinthians 10:31), waking or sleeping (or, for that matter, dreaming), in work and leisure, in the gathered community of the Lord's people and scattered in the world. When we gather in local churches for worship, we bring into focus in God's presence all we do; it's something like an aircraft getting a 'fine tune'. We do not 'come to worship' to 'withdraw from the world'; rather we bring all we do in the world into the presence of the Lord as an offering to him.

The focus is on the Lord, so let's get the attention off ourselves. We worship him because it is our duty to do so, and in response to all he has done for us. And worship — serving the Lord — is much more than 'going to preaching'. (The most common question asked by someone who 'missed church' in Western countries: 'what did he say?'). Would you describe your church's worship as service of the Lord? Is that its main orientation?

Wesley described the essence of worship in one of his hymns as being 'lost in wonder, love and praise'. It's interesting that when I ask Christians how often they are lost in wonder, love and praise in their worship they look bemused or sad: it's a rare experience for most of them (less rare, interestingly, for those at the liturgical or the charismatic ends of the worship spectrum: these two groups, broadly speaking, have captured the grandeur of Christian tradition on the one hand and the beauty of freedom in worship on the other).

Leading worship

It is very important that the worship leader should be worshipping too. Sometimes worship leaders think that by scolding ('C'mon, get with it! You can sing better than that!') they are facilitating worship: the reverse is most probably true. The leader ought not to shuffle papers, or peer over the hymnbook to see who's present or absent while the people of God are singing a serious hymn of praise! As I travel from church to church, I find the more filled up with God the people are, the less prompting is needed from 'up front'. 'The demeanour of the worship leader and the congregation should transmit the message that here is a meeting of extraordinary importance. When it comes to leading worship the unforgivable sin is to be flippant or sloppy.' (Stan Stewart, 'Q: When is Worship Good for Children? A: When it's Good for Everyone'.)[2]. J. S. Whale warned, 'Instead of putting off our shoes because the place whereon we stand is holy ground, we like to take nice photographs of the burning bush from suitable angles'.[3]

This reminds me of something I heard Lyle Schaller say: 'The most critical formative factor in children's coming to faith is their perception that what the Big People are doing in their worship and learning experiences is vital, alive, enjoyable, and very, very important'.

So for the pastor and or worship-leader, the key question is not 'What can I do before these people that will be judged by them as excellent?' It is 'How can I enable them to do high business with God?' These are utterly different agendas. It's the difference between being a coach and being the star player. 'If you go to worship and all you leave with are certain evaluations of how the worship leaders have performed, you have missed the main point of that enterprise.'[4]

Discuss one or more of the following: (1) Read Isaiah 6:1-9 and Psalm 8:3–9. Describe how the worshipper feels in each instance. What prompted, and what was significant about his response? (2) Read through Psalm 96. Notice how worship is recognising the greatness and power of God (v. 8); worship expressed in different ways — singing (v. 1), preaching: telling others about God (v. 2), giving (v. 8), and prayer: the whole psalm is a prayer. Notice the reverence, 'honour' we give to God (v. 4), but we are not afraid of him, because he will treat us with justice and mercy (v. 13). (3) Look at Isaiah 1:10–17 and Micah 6:6–8. What do these Scriptures indicate about God's displeasure with worship divorced from justice? (4) How should the psalms be used in Christian worship — particularly the ones that extol war and retribution? (5) Compare and contrast these two hymns: 'And now, O Father mindful of the love' and 'I come to the garden alone'.

Further Reading: Richard Foster. *Celebration of Discipline*, London: Hodder & Stoughton, 1978, chapter 11 'Worship'; William Willimon & Robert L. Wilson. *Preaching and Worship in the Small Church,* Nashville: Abingdon, 1980; James F. White. *Introduction to Christian Worship*, Nashville: Abingdon, 1980; John Gunstone. *A People for his Praise*, London: Hodder & Stoughton, 1978.

NOTES

1 Frederick Buechner, *Wishful Thinking: a Theological ABC*, London: Collins, 1973, p. 97.
2 *On Being*, March 1984, p. 22.
3 Quoted in many places, including Ken Manley, 'Worship — changes or not?', *The Australian Baptist*, date unknown).
4 John Claypool, 'The challenge of ministry today', (unpublished transcript of an address given to a pastor's conference at Southwestern Baptist Theological Seminary, June 25, 1974).

29

Fasting is healthy!

Fasting is abstaining from eating, or another legitimate activity, for religious purposes. Jews fasted on the Day of Atonement (Leviticus 16:29–31; 23:26–32; Numbers 29:7–11), and for other special reasons such as mourning (1 Samuel 31:13), after defeat in battle (1 Samuel 7:6), as a sign of repentance or remorse (2 Samuel 12:15–23, Joel 2:12-13), and to accompany intercession (Nehemiah 1, 4).

Jesus fasted during his wilderness preparation for ministry (Matthew 4:1–2, Luke 4:1–2), but said only two things about fasting in his teaching in the gospels: it was an act of private devotion to God, and was appropriate once he left his followers (Matthew 6:16–18, 9:14–15; cf. Mark 2:18–20; Luke 5:33–35). The apostolic church apparently observed fasts during times of solemn commitment (Acts 13:2–3, 14:23).

Fasting is 'praying with the body', an affirmation of one's hunger for God and his will, an act of spiritual discipline, and an assertion of the goodness of God in creation, which one appreciates better in abstention; it

> expresses penitence for the rejection and crucifixion of Christ by the human race; it is a following of Jesus on his way of fasting; it is one element in mortification; the acceptance of death of self in the death of Christ, and thereby an act of faith in the resurrection.[1]

Fasting has its dangers, when misused for selfish ends. The Bible notes such abuses as fasting as a means of getting things from God (manipulation or magic); it can be a substitute for genuine repentance and be formalistic; it can be masochistic — an exaggerated self-denial; psychological evidence shows fasting can sometimes lead to self-induced visions which may not be helpful.[2]

So, in summary, there are no biblical laws that command regular fasting, but, as Martin Luther said, 'It was not Christ's intention to reject or despise fasting ... it was his intention to restore proper fasting'. It is clear that Christ both upheld the discipline of fasting and anticipated that his followers would do it.[3]

Further Reading: Richard Foster. *Celebration of Discipline*. San Francisco: Harper & Row, 1978; Arthur Wallis. *God's Chosen Fast.* CLC, 1986; Joseph F. Wemmer. *Fasting in the New Testament.* New York: Paulist Press, 1982.

NOTES

1 David Tripp, 'Fasting' in Wakefield, Gordon S. (ed.), *A Dictionary of Christian Spirituality*, London: SCM, 1983, p. 148.

2 R. D. Linder, 'Fasting', in Elwell, (ed.), *Evangelical Dictionary of Theology*, Michigan: Baker Book House, 1984, pp. 406–7.

3 Richard Foster, *Celebration of Discipline*, London: Hodder & Stoughton, 1980, chapter 4. I heard Richard Foster give a lecture at Fuller Seminary on fasting where he suggested fasting from such entities as the telephone, billboards, television and other things — any deprivation that may get our means and ends into perspective for a while.

30

On listening to the Holy Spirit

There was an interesting minute on the books of the church at Antioch: while they were meeting together 'serving the Lord and fasting' the Holy Spirit spoke to them (Acts 13:2). Now I can't ever remember a minute like that in any ecclesiastical meeting I've attended! So here are some challenging questions: How did the Holy Spirit speak to this church? How often does the Holy Spirit 'speak' to your church in its worship? How does he speak? What does he say?

'All the great figures in Acts are people of the Spirit', writes William Barclay.

Filled with the Spirit, Peter addressed the sanhedrin (4:8). When there was a need for new workers, the instruction was to seek out seven men of honest report and full of the Spirit (6:3). Stephen was full of faith and the Holy Spirit (6:5) ... Paul was filled with the Holy Spirit at the beginning of his ministry for Christ (9:17, 13:8). Barnabas was a good man, full of the Holy Spirit and faith (11:24). The criterion by which the early church judged a person was that person's relationship to the Holy Spirit ... It is even said of Jesus himself that God anointed him with the Holy Spirit and with power (10:38) ... Had it not been for the guidance of the Spirit, the church might well have remained nothing more than a sect of Judaism ... The real test of a church lies not in the statistics which an ecclesiastical yearbook can convey, but in the presence or absence of the Spirit.[1]

One of the saddest things that can happen to churches over time is that they become institutionalised. There is something inherent within every religious and political movement as it tends towards inertia, dogmatism and legalism. In his brilliant book *The Go-Between God*, John V. Taylor notes that spiritual growth does not come 'from hearing and submitting to extraneous regulation ... Where Christians are still thinking in the traditional ways, they may ... grow less and less distinctively Christian'. Spiritual dynamism comes from trusting the Holy Spirit rather than an imposed discipline.[2]

The Pharisees will always be with us. From motives of protecting the accoutrements of the faith from contamination, they imprison it within structures and laws and dogma. So the church becomes throttled in its own institutionalism. 'Listening to the Spirit' is replaced by listening to the constitution, or tradition, or creed. It's only in the young churches (like Antioch in the first century, and many third world churches in our times) that you find a minute like this one.

Jurgen Moltman makes the same point. It is easy, he says, for a church to settle down into a comfortable orthodoxy, with decision-making structures in place, constitutions formulated, activities planned for this or that purpose, and all we are doing is rearranging old wine-skins. Or we reduce salvation to justification by faith and forget that 'through justification the unjust person is led into the history of the Spirit ... becomes obedient in hope and the practice of divine righteousness ... Liberation leads to the liberated life. Justification leads to the new creation'.[3]

The picture often used to describe this state of affairs is that of opening of the church's windows. The fresh wind of the Spirit comes into the stuffy place and blows all the papers around. The elders scurry about collecting them again, organise everything as before, and close the windows. So the Spirit takes his leave ...

Discuss: It is very difficult to fight institutionalism. How do you plan to do it in your church?

NOTES

1 William Barclay, *The Promise of the Spirit*, London: Epworth, 1960, pp. 55 ff.

2 John V. Taylor, *The Go-Between God: The Holy Spirit and the Christian Mission*, London: SCM, 1972, p. 159.

3 Jurgen Moltmann, *The Church in the Power of the Spirit*, London: SCM, 1977, p. 36.

31

Ministry as empowerment

What an astonishing thing for the Holy Spirit to suggest to the Antioch church: 'I want your two key leaders!' Apparently they had by now 'worked themselves out of a job' by training people to take their place.

We now embark on one of the most crucial journeys in this book, beginning with an introduction to 'ethology'.

Ethology is the study of the comparison between human and animal behaviour. An important concept in ethology is the notion of territoriality: the practice of marking a piece of ground and defending it against intruders.[1] Animals as diverse as fish, worms, gazelles and lizards stake out particular areas and put up fierce resistance when intruders encroach on their area. Many species use odorous secretions to mark the boundaries of their territory. For example the wolf marks its domain by urinating around the perimeter.

Some scholars argue that people are territorial animals: humans' genetic endowment drive them to gain and defend territory, much as other animals do. 'The dog barking at you from behind his master's fence acts for a motive indistinguishable from that of his master when the fence was built.'[2] The list of territorial behaviours is endless: in a library you protect your space with a book, coat or notebook; you 'save a place' in the theatre or at the beach — reserving a spot that is 'mine' or 'ours'; juvenile gangs fight to protect their turf; neighbours of similar ethnic backgrounds join forces to keep other groups out; nations war over contested territory; and, between churches, pastors accuse other pastors of 'sheep-stealing'.[3]

Our own personal territory may include our room, specific seats in a class or in church, a particular table at the restaurant ... The more attached you are to an area, the more likely you are to signal your 'ownership' with obvious territorial markers such as decorations, plants, photographs, posters or even graffiti. College dorms and business offices are prime places to observe this type of territorial marking.

As a result of our fallenness, this planet and its inhabitants have substituted 'territoriality' ('my space — keep out') for 'hospitality' ('my space — you're welcome!'). Throughout the Bible we have numerous stories and injunctions about reversing this effect of the Fall. You know them — references to prophets' chambers, looking after aliens, opening our homes to strangers and entertaining angels unawares, being hospitable to one another, prophetically denouncing the group which does not welcome Jesus' messengers, Jesus being a stranger and we take him in, and so on.

Now pastors and leaders in the church are invited to be 'hospitable' rather than 'territorial', and it's something they generally do very poorly. The biblical models are clear. Moses was told by his father-in-law: 'You're killing yourself!' (Exodus 18:18). In essence his good advice to Moses was: your task is to pray for these people to God; teach them God's laws; and appoint others as co-leaders. When Jesus was recruiting disciples to lead his church he had the same three priorities: prayer, teaching (by instruction and modelling), and training for ministry. It's amazing how much Jesus delegated to his disciples so early in their relationship: 'Go and preach, heal the sick, bring the dead back to life ... drive out demons' (Matthew 10:5–8). Just the simple stuff, fellows, to start with!

Then when these apostles messed up the early church's social welfare system, they had an 'aha' experience: 'Oh, we should have remembered; our task is to give our full time to prayer, and preaching, so let's delegate other ministries to people full of the Holy Spirit and wisdom' (Acts 6:1–4). It would be wonderful if more pastors had this kind of 'aha' experience.

Now why don't they? Fasten your seat-belts: this paragraph will contain some turbulence. The devil could not get Jesus to accrue power to himself (Matthew 4:1–11; 16:21–28) so he has tried the same temptations on the shepherds of Jesus' church. And he has generally succeeded. The church very early in its institutional history developed an 'official' ministry which separated 'ordained' Christians from others. These 'priests' alone had sacramental prerogatives. The Protestant Reformers rejected Roman Catholic and Orthodox theology and practice at this point, but, in my view, did not take their reformation far enough. Protestant pastors generally feel that they, too, control certain prerogatives in the life of the church (presiding at most sacramental observances, preaching most of the sermons, blessing most of the meetings, etc.), and are reluctant to share these ministries with others. They have perhaps forgotten that their key role is equipping (Ephesians 4:12), empowering others for ministry, not doing it all themselves as paid 'professional employees' of the church.

Frankly, it's nice having these privileges: all the clergy surveys tell us they enjoy these public roles in most cases. Taking power to ourselves is the devil's primal trick however. Justice, we said, is essentially about power. When we deny others their empowering, that's unjust.

To change the metaphor, let us transform the classical 'wheel-model' of the church — where all the spokes centre on one person or small leadership group — to a discipling model. Pastor-teachers ought to spend more time with fewer people, training them for leadership and ministry on the job.

So, back to Antioch. The acid test for ministry-leaders at this point is: how hard have you trained others? Could you leave your church after one year, as Paul and Barnabas did, safely in the hands of those you have prepared for leadership in ministry? Do you take people with you as you visit folk? Do you run courses on how to help your friend, how to lead a small group, on how to grow as a Christian? How about your church becoming a miniature theological seminary, as Elton Trueblood suggests? That is, how about doing in your congregation what Jesus did with his disciples? Or what Paul suggests Timothy do: 'Take the teachings ... and entrust them to reliable people, who will teach others also' (2 Timothy 2:2). Well?

Exercise: Pastors: do the 'Ministry Empowerment Questionnaire' (see appendix), and then discuss your findings with the elders and leaders of the church.

Further Reading: Robert Greenleaf. *Servant Leadership: A Journey into the Nature of Legitimate Power and Greatness.* New York: Paulist Press, 1977; James Fenhagen. *Mutual Ministry: New Vitality for the Local Church.* New York: Seabury, 1977; Carnegie Samuel Calian. *Today's Pastor in Tomorrow's World.* Philadelphia: Westminster, 1977, 1982; George Peck and John S. Hoffman, (eds), *The Laity in Ministry: The Whole People of God for the Whole World.* Valley Forge: Judson Press, 1984; R. Paul Stevens. *Liberating the Laity: Equipping all the Saints for Ministry.* Illinois: InterVarsity Press, 1985; Douglas W. Johnson. *The Care and Feeding of Volunteers.* Nashville: Abingdon, 1978.

NOTES

1 See J. L. Freedman, *Crowding and Behavior*, New York: Viking Press, 1975.

2 For example R. Ardrey, *The Territorial Imperative*, New York: Atheneum, 1966, p.5.

3 On the notion of 'sheep-stealing' as territorial behaviour see Lyle Schaller, *Effective Church Planning*, Nashville: Abingdon, 1979, chapter 2 'The Importance of Place', pp. 65 ff. For an interesting discussion of 'parish' as territorial behaviour, see Andrew Greeley, *Confessions of a Parish Priest*, New York: Pocket Books, 1987, pp. 81f.

32

Christians who pray together . . .

'So they fasted [again!] and prayed' (Acts 13:3). Prayer is to spirituality what eating is to hunger. Prayer is the 'soul of faith' (John Calvin).

Biblical prayer includes adoration, being 'lost in wonder, love and praise'; confession: if we confess our sins, God will forgive (1 John 1:9), and it is sometimes helpful to confess our sins to one another (James 5:16); intercession, (work-in-prayer for others); petition: asking God for things in Christ's name — i.e., praying for the things Christ would pray for; thanksgiving (for what God has done) and praise (for who God is).

Here in essence is what the ancient and modern masters of prayer teach us:
- Pray as you can, not as you can't: your own relationship with God will be unique.
- Ask yourself 'What is my desire?' (Mark 11:24): be honest and clear about what you want from God.
- Prayer is a gift from God, not a bag of spiritual techniques: it is not so much you who are looking for God, but he who is searching for fellowship with you.
- The main aim of prayer is to know God, through love.

- There are three kinds of praying — with words, with guided thoughts (meditation), and with wonder (contemplation).
- Find a quiet, regular place and time for prayer every day: if possible, try to be unhurried and uninterrupted.
- Prayer is also living and working (see Isaiah 1:15–17).[1]

The most compelling reason for praying with others is Jesus' promise that 'whenever two of you on earth agree about anything you pray for, it will be done for you by my Father in heaven. For where two or three come together in my Name, I am there with them' (Matthew 18:19, 20).

Jesus took his disciples with him occasionally when he was praying in solitary places (Luke 9:18,28). We know what Jesus prayed in Gethsemane probably because part of his prayer was overheard (Mark 14:33).

The apostolic Christians prayed together from the start. The Holy Spirit was poured out on a group at prayer (Acts 1:14). They continued to spend a lot of time in prayer together (Acts 2:42). Paul prayed constantly with his co-missioners (Colossians 1:9; 1 Thessalonians 1:2; 2 Thessalonians 1:11) and asked others to join him in disciplined prayer (Romans 15:30). James (5:16) tells us to 'confess your sins to one another and pray for one another, so that you will be healed'.

Praying together is one of the richest experiences Christians can have with each other. 'There is a deep joy in praying together, an added vitality, a plus difficult to define. It is rather like the difference between eating your meal alone and sharing in a party feast. Eating together is not the same as eating in solitude; the something more is the company, the fellowship. So it is with prayer.'[2]

But prayer with others is not only helpful to us, it is also associated with all the great spiritual awakenings. For example, the Evangelical Revival in England in the late 18th century began in a little 'Holy Club' at Oxford. So impressed were the Wesleys with the prayer cell principle that every Methodist society was organised into small Band and Class meetings. Similarly the great revival in America in 1857–1858 was empowered and nurtured in prayer meetings. The longest-lasting revival in Christian history, affecting five generations of Koreans, has been noted for its powerful prayer meetings.

In his books *How to Develop A Praying Church* and *The Exciting Church Where People Really Pray*, Charlie Shedd lists the advantages of praying with others. In a chapter in the latter book entitled 'Where the People Pray — These Good Things Happen' he lists these 'good things': 'They care for each other; lives will be changed; they attract new members; there will be social concern; they also serve the church; they reach out to the world; the little negatives stay little; everyone is able to serve'.[3]

For some evangelical churches the question 'should we have a prayer meeting for the whole church once a week or meet in small groups?' is an issue. The guiding principle is clear: corporate prayer happens best where there is a sense of community.

In most churches (especially larger churches with multiple worship services) the small group is the place for real community. In small parishes, particularly in rural areas, the whole church could meet for prayer. Probably, however, the small group ought to be the norm, especially in cities and suburbs. This gives opportunities for fathers and mothers to be involved at separate times if they have small children, and young people to learn from their peers (although they ought also to meet from time to time in trans-generational groups as well).

A whole church prayer meeting is most appropriate when there is a strong call for such across the congregation (e.g. at times of crisis, or special events). Experience around the world is now teaching us that more people will pray more meaningfully in small groups than in larger ones.

Such 'growth groups', 'prayer cells' — call them what you will — should do three things: Scripture reading, meditation and study; sharing of our personal concerns with one another; then prayer. That is, we listen to God, listen to each other, then speak to God the things that have arisen in the other two encounters. The 'mix' of Bible, sharing and prayer will vary from group to group, and from time to time in one group. What is important is that all three occur in all groups all the time.

Ideas for Group Prayer

Here's a pot-pourri of principles and suggestions for praying with others:

- The best size for the group will depend on what it does. If the emphasis is on personal sharing or therapy, it ought to be small — say 3 to 6. If the group majors on Bible discussion the optimum size is 8 to 12. If it's a 'house church' there may be 30 to 40, but there ought to be times where 'twos or threes' pray together.
- Sensitivity ought to be shown towards those who have rarely, if ever, prayed aloud before. Ease them into it by encouraging written prayers to be read, sentence prayers to be spoken, or 'prayer points' shared which one or two may bring to God on behalf of the group. With acceptance and love and encouragement,

it ought to be expected that all will soon be able to pray aloud. The lengthy prayers of the verbose might have to be 'reined in' in the process!
• There aren't many books on group prayer, and few resources. However, some excellent material can be found in John Mallison's *Learning and Praying* (Vol. 2 in his series on small groups), and Maxie Dunnam's *The Workbook of Living Prayer*. Charles Kemp's *Prayer-based Growth Groups* (Abingdon) is a good introduction.

Many Approaches

• There are many ways to pray together. Charlie Shedd says 'Pray in your own way. There are twelve gates into the holy city and a thousand different doors to prayer. When we pray we are entering a vast expanse of truth which leaves room for much experiment and many approaches'.
• Being silent in a group is important. After the Scripture is read it is good to encourage silent meditation on the sacred words for a few minutes — or longer. 'For people who live hectic lives, corporate meditation can be an oasis in a desert.'[4] Silent retreats, or quiet days with others can be healing occasions.[5]
• Sometimes the group can devote time to adoration and praise. Confession can happen in a group by silently writing down our sins, tearing the paper into small pieces, passing a cup around, then enacting absolution (either by saying something like 'As you have confessed your sins to God, in the name of Jesus you are forgiven' to one another in turn; or by the leader on behalf of the group). Thanksgiving can follow this experience. Bidding prayers can invite members to verbalise their blessing. (For example: 'let us recall "high moments" from the recent past; let us thank God for someone, a book we have read, a Scripture that has been meaningful to us', etc.). Specific intercession, selfless prayers for others, ought to be written down as they are prayed (to check for God's answer). Sometimes it is enough to mention a name, and no more details (to avoid gossip). Trust and confidentiality are important here. The group prayer could conclude with someone bringing a special benediction; or by the group praying a written-out prayer of dedication.
• Try one- or two-word prayers of adoration: 'Jesus', 'Father', 'maranatha', 'Lord, you are here', etc. Sometimes write out a litany, or pray a great hymn of adoration or dedication together. Bidding prayers can be offered by group members ('Let us pray for our pastor and elders'; 'Let us uphold our prime minister and cabinet before God'). Pluriform praying — all praying aloud at the same

time — is practised in many cultures, and over many centuries. It's beautiful once we overcome our initial embarrassment!

• The 'laying on of hands' if someone has a special need (or by proxy for someone else) is an ancient practice being revived in many churches today. Symbols and liturgies have, from time immemorial, enriched the church's worship. Those of us from the 'Free churches' who are exploring these riches are finding treasures everywhere! For example, a cross, candle, loaf of bread, chalice, jug of water, open Bible, vacant chair, or a simple drawing of a fish or a dove, and other traditional symbols can be useful aids if they are varied.[6]

Group prayer is an act of fellowship building up the body of Christ in love; it is a ministry of care and support to fellow Christians; a participation together in mission beyond local or regional boundaries; and an expression of life and relationship to Christ.[7]

Discuss: How many in your church are praying regularly with others? What might be done to increase this number?

Further Reading: Dietrich Bonhoeffer, *Life Together*, San Francisco: Harper & Row, 1954; Sheila Cassidy, *Prayer for Pilgrims*, London: Collins, 1980. Richard Foster, *Celebration of Discipline*, London: Hodder & Stoughton, 1980; John Mallison, *Growing Christians in Small Groups*, Melbourne: JBCE, 1989; Rowland Croucher (ed.), *Still Waters Deep Waters: Meditations and Prayers for Busy People*, Sydney: Albatross, 1987. *High Mountains Deep Valleys: More Meditations and Prayers for Busy People*, Sydney: Albatross, 1990.

NOTES

1 Rowland Croucher, *Recent Trends Among Evangelicals*, Part 3: 'Creative Spirituality', Sydney: Albatross, 1986, pp. 59ff.

2 Stephen Winward, *Teach Yourself to Pray*, Hodder & Stoughton, p. 86.

3 Quoted in John Mallison, *Learning and Praying*, Renewal Publications, 1976, p. 133.

4 Michael Wright, *New Ways for Christ*, Mowbrays, 1975, p. 44.

5 See, e.g. Margaret Harvey, *Worship and Silence*, Grove Books, 1975.

6 Mallison, op. cit., p. 167.

7 Frank Akehurst, *Praying Aloud Together*, Grove Books, 1975, p. 20.

33

Commissioning for ministry

The main point we are making here about ordination for ministry is that everyone's in it! Every Christian is ordained for ministry (at baptism).

Edward Schillebeeckx writes:

There is no mention in the New Testament of an essential distinction between 'laity' and 'ministers' ... the ministry is not a status, but a function. For the New Testament, the essential apostolic structure of the community and therefore of the ministry of its leaders has nothing to do with what is called the 'hierarchical' structure of the church. (The coming community of the church) is a community in which the power structures which prevail in the world are gradually broken down. All have responsibility, though there are functional differences ...[1]

He also states: '(this is not to deny the special role of) team leader(s) who coordinate(s) all charismatic services ... I am opposed to a view which appears here and there, that any believer at all can preside at the eucharist even when leaders of the community ('priests') are present.'[2]

It would be at that point that Schillebeeckx and I would disagree. Who leads the community in sacramental offices was, I think, not a great concern for the early church; Paul could not remember who baptised whom at Corinth (1 Corinthians 1:14-16). This is, however, not a denial of pastoral leadership as such. It is simply saying that faithful leaders in the Christian community will model their ministry on that of Jesus, who trained his followers in every aspect of service, and allowed them the freedom to exercise those ministries, even when he was around. Perhaps Schillebeeckx's thinking on this question moved a little in my direction by the time his *The Church With a Human Face* was published five years later. There he writes:

> The early eucharist was structured after the pattern of Jewish grace at meals ... at which just anyone could preside ... The general conception is that anyone *who is competent to lead the community* (emphasis mine) in one way or another is ipso facto also president at the eucharist (and in this sense presiding at the eucharist does not need any separate authorisation). The New Testament does not tell us *any more than this*' (again, emphasis mine).[3]

Once the community has recognised 'who is competent to lead', such persons ought to be commissioned for their ministries. This can be done at a special service, by the 'laying on of hands' (hands belonging to representatives from the congregation, not necessarily those of the 'heavies' present!). I would encourage the commissioning, from time to time, of everyone who has a recognised ministry within the church body.

Discuss: Do you agree with the above? How can you implement this general idea in your church?

NOTES

1 Edward Schillebeeckx, *Ministry: A Case for Change*, London: SCM, 1981, pp. 21, 135.

2 Ibid, pp. 135, 139.

3 Edward Schillebeeckx, *The Church With a Human Face*, SCM, 1985, pp. 119-20.

34

The world is your parish

Every healthy church regards the world as their parish (as John Wesley put it). Churches that are not concerned for mission are dying. Some missiologists refer to the 'choke law': once a church is established, pastoral and administrative work tends to choke out continuing evangelisation. The church becomes institutionalised and static, rather than mission-oriented and dynamic.

As we have already emphasised, biblical mission involves three concerns: compassion for those the New Testament calls the lost (evangelism); compassion for the hurting (mercy) and compassion for the powerless (justice). These three concerns are highlighted by Micah (6:8) and Jesus (Matthew 23:23) as being essential to an authentic biblical faith. Mission in the Bible involves three modes: word (what we say to others for God); deed (what we do for others in the Lord's name); and sign (what God does to corroborate his Word through our words and his works through our deeds).

A church with a well-balanced missionary program — balanced geographically between 'home' or local community ministries, and 'overseas' or foreign missions, and also between the various components of mission, justice, mercy and evangelism — is likely to be a healthy church.

There aren't too many of them. I have known 'missionary churches' which were not too concerned about the needs of people in their own vicinity. Then, too, there are many congregations who don't have home-grown overseas missionaries in their prayers and budgets. Conservative churches have their 'gospel meetings' (preaching mostly to the already committed) but aren't concerned about biblical justice. 'Mainline' churches may have study groups to look at justice issues, but have ignored the 'lostness' of people without Christ. Other churches have many volunteers to run Thrift Shops, or Meals-on-Wheels, but can't name any recent converts, and aren't about to 'get political'.

It's the devil's job to polarise churches in all these areas, making them exclusive to one another. It's the Spirit's quest to unite all these mission elements. And healthy churches, as we said above, are 'listening to the Spirit'.

Discuss: How can your church begin to implement a program of wholistic, biblical mission? For example, is each group in the church encouraged to have an evangelistic, mercy and justice aim?

Further Reading: Vincent Donovan, *Christianity Rediscovered*, London: SCM, 1982; John V. Taylor, *The Go-Between God: The Holy Spirit and Christian Mission*, London: SCM, 1972. Donal Dorr, *Spirituality and Justice*, Dublin: Gill and Macmillan, 1984.

* * * * *

• The church I dream about is working on all these thirty-four fronts. As we said earlier, the church at Antioch is meant to be a model, for any church in any place at any time. The principles are all there, and they are contemporary for us too. Let us, in the power of the Spirit, create communities of faith and love and hope, which will show the world the power of the Good News.

To God be glory in the church ... ! (Ephesians 3:21).

Photo: New Times

Postscript
Live in hope: your church can come alive!

The pastor of a dynamic church in England was preaching about the wonderful opportunities all around their parish. His text: Deuteronomy 1:19 ff.- 'Look, there is the land. Go and occupy it as the Lord your God commanded. Do not hesitate or be afraid. The Lord your God will lead you'. To press his point he gave out 800 seedless grapes to the people (seedless in deference to the caretaker!). 'God is leading us!' he preached that day. 'Men and women of faith — lead, conquer, win — take these grapes to others!'

Life for the people of God is pilgrimage, sojourn, movement. The church should be taking more territory — not merely holding on to what we've got and defending it. The enemy of the church wants us to be fearful, to gear down to neutral, to move from the developmental to a maintenance mode.

This is part of what the Bible means by 'living in hope'. 'My hope is in the Lord' was the Psalmists' confident affirmation. 'Hope' or its equivalents are mentioned 125 times in Scripture — often linked with faith and love (1 Corinthians 13:13, Colossians 1:4,5, 1 Thessalonians 1:3, Hebrews 10:22–24).

Earlier in this book we discussed two kinds of faith. One of these — *'fides'* faith — includes an ingredient of optimism. Now we have to say that just as biblical faith is more than optimism, so is biblical hope. The New Testament talks about the 'patience of hope'. Christian hope is deep; mere optimism may be shallow. Optimism may be a good natural trait — and have no religious connections at all. 'Hope', says John Macquarrie in his little book *The Humility of God* (SCM Press, London, 1978), 'is humble, trustful, vulnerable. Optimism is arrogant, brash, complacent ... Our hope is not that in spite of everything we do, all will turn out for the best. Our hope is rather that God is with us and ahead of us, opening a way in which we can responsibly follow'.

Hope is not conditional upon trouble being removed. Hope means God is with us in trouble and in triumph. Resurrection hope means God is with us in life and death. Hope means the God who was with his people in the past will be with them always.

Hope is a primal human need. Viktor Frankl was a young psychiatrist who had just begun his practice when the Germans took over his native Vienna and shipped him and his fellow Jews off to a concentration camp. Then began the awesome task of survival. With his trained psychiatric eye he noted that many prisoners simply crumpled under the pressure and eventually died. But some did not, and Frankl made it his mission to get to know these special people and discover their secret. Without exception, those who survived had something to live for. One man had a retarded child back home he wanted to care for. Another was deeply in love with a girl he wanted to marry. Frankl himself aspired to be a writer, and was in the middle of his first manuscript when he was arrested: the drive to live and finish the book was very great. Frankl did survive, and has contributed greatly to our understanding of the human 'will to meaning'. He developed a process called 'logotherapy', which, expressed as a simple question is: 'If the presence of purpose or meaning gives one the strength to carry on, how do we human beings get it touch with it?'

The Bible's answer — for an individual or a church — is, in one word, HOPE. Human persons are 'hopeful beings'. Where there's hope there's life. That's because our God is a 'God of hope' (Romans 15:13); those who do not know God are 'without hope' (Ephesians 2:12).

Once when Martin Luther was feeling depressed, his wife asked if he had heard God had died. Luther replied angrily that she was blaspheming. She retorted that if God had indeed not died, what right had he to be despondent and without hope!

Hope, says Martin Buber, is 'imagining the real'. It is not fantasy or wishful thinking — like Mr Micawber's 'hoping that something will turn up'. It's not 'she'll be right mate'! Hope deals with imagining possibilities, then having the faith to work hard to see those possibilities realised.

Let me give you an example. When ethnic families move into a previously 'white anglo-saxon' area, many churches die. The reason is simple: like the dinosaurs, these churches fail to adapt. They want things to stay the same for two reasons — selfishness (the church is their social club and they don't want strangers in it), or fear (they don't know how to communicate to these 'new people'). So they suffer from 'ethnikitis', a potentially fatal disease for a church.

But some churches remain healthy in these contexts. They begin by seeing possibilities: these newcomers are generally quite lonely. People on the move are excellent prospects for evangelisation. (Most people converted in the Book of Acts were away from home!) They've had their roots torn up, and are ready for replanting in a new community. So a Baptist church in Melbourne runs parallel programs for Cambodians, and incorporates some

Kampuchean-language readings and prayers, songs and a benediction into their combined Sunday morning service. Another church in Sydney sponsored a Greek pastor to reach out to Greek-speaking peoples. Many churches throughout Australia have Vietnamese congregations.

Or take another group — the deaf. Working with deaf people is a difficult, challenging ministry, but many American precedents show it can be very rewarding. It takes patience, skilled interpreters (note the plural), and some dedicated people (again, note the plural) willing to give a lot of time to pastoring the deaf and their families. Eventually, such hard work will pay off, and the front right-hand rows of your church-building will be regularly occupied with these special, suffering people.

So, as Robert Schuller titled one of his books, 'Your Church Has Real Possibilities!' Go to it, with God! Your church can come alive!

Bible Study: Using 1 Peter 1:1–9 as your text, develop a sermon/study on the subject of hope. Here are some suggested headings: biblical hope is certain, living, a resurrection hope, and it's practical. Study the background of this epistle: to whom was the author writing about hope? What might have been their circumstances? How can we be encouraged to 'live in hope'?

Appendix
In search of pastoral excellence: A ministry empowerment questionnaire

Pastor-teachers 'prepare God's people for Christian service, in order to build up the body of Christ', so that they may become 'mature people' (Ephesians 4:12,13). How well are you doing?

Answer every question by circling the appropriate number (1) (2) (3) (4) or (5). If in doubt, choose the most nearly correct answer. Note: 'Practical theology' is all about the practice of ministry, and covers such areas as the theology of ministry, spirituality for ministry/mission, preaching, Christian education/formation, counselling, church leadership, Christian management, etc.

1. Preparation
To equip myself to equip others I spend time in prayer, reflection and study each week: (1) 20+ hours (2) 15–19 hours (3) 10–14 hours (4) 5–9 hours (5) Less than 5 hours.

2. Delegation
As a pastor-leader, I would delegate at least three or four pastoral visits to others each week; I do not attend most committees in the church but keep in touch with them indirectly; I live comfortably with the idea that people other than I can chair significant church meetings or committees; I am not worried if I do not know the details of everything that happens in the church; when a job has to be done, I have a habit of asking myself 'Am I the best person to do it? Would I be depriving someone else of a ministry if I did it?'; I readily delegate tasks to others; most of the time I have the skill to choose the right persons for a job, and am happy to leave them with it; I circulate leadership material (e.g. World Vision's *GRID*) to all our leaders. (1) I would score well in all these areas (2) OK in four or more of them (3) three (4) two (5) one or none.

3. Formal theological training
(1) 4+ years full-time or equivalent (2) 3–4 years full-time or equivalent (3) 2–3 years full-time or equivalent (4) 1–2 years full-time or equivalent (5) Less than one year.

4. Practical theology
My theological training included practical theology components such as • regular spiritual direction with a spiritual guide, • personal growth and development, • a supervised pastoral placement, • a thorough critique of my communication/preaching skills, • supervised counselling, • a time management course, • leadership skill development, • other courses in practical theology: (1) all of these (2) at least four of these (3) three (4) two (5) one or none.

5. Continuing education
I do a post-seminary course (of at least 3 days' duration) in some area of practical theology (1) more than once a year (2) about once a year (3) less than once a year (4) about every 2–3 years (5) hardly ever.

6. Professional reading
I read books on practical theology: (1) at least one a week (2) about 2–3 a month (3) about 1–2 a month (4) about 1–2 every two months (5) fewer than 1–2 every three months.

7. Journals
I read practical ministry periodicals or journals: (1) 4 or more a month (2) about 3 a month (3) about 2 a month (4) about one a month (5) fewer than one a month.

8. Leadership training
• I would meet with key leaders individually at least once a month; • I meet with the leadership team for a training session at least once a month; • these leaders would aim to reproduce themselves in the lives of others; • we have elders who visit members on a regular basis; • we have commissioned deaconesses or lay visitors who visit in homes and hospitals; • at least 10% of our regular Sunday attenders would be involved in significant occasional counselling of others in need; • there is a 'prayer chain' or similar structure to engage in intercessory prayer for those in difficulty; • we have regular community ministries in place that would meaningfully contact the equivalent of at least 20% of our Sunday attendance each week; • at least a quarter of our people would know how to pray with someone to receive Christ as Saviour and Lord; • a significant minority of our people would find themselves spontaneously praying with another as part of a meaningful contact. (1) We would score well in at least seven of the above (2) five-six (3) three-four (4) one or two (5) none.

9. Worship leadership
Our church involves many people in leading worship services through • seminars on worship; • setting up one or more worship committees; • having at least two people participate in leadership besides the preacher in most worship services; • involving musically gifted people to help choose hymns/songs; • training persons with preaching/teaching skills and allowing them to minister publicly according to their gifts; • opening up a part of many services for people to share their faith stories. We do (1) all of these (2) four of them (3) three (4) two (5) one or none of the above.

10. Counselling training
There is a 'counseling/how to help your friend' course run by our church (or some other nearby group which our church members are urged to attend): (1) about once a year (2) about once every 2 years (3) about once every 3 years (4) every 4 years or so (5) never or hardly ever.

11. Visitation training
To train people in visitation/counselling I have a trainee with me (1) at least 50% of my people-time (2) 30–40% (3) 20–30% (4) 10–20% (5) Less than 10%.

12. Growth groups
The proportion of our regular Sunday attenders belonging at any one time to a small group for spiritual growth would be (1) 70% or more (2) 45–70% (3) 25–45% (4) 10–25% (5) less than 10%.

13. Formation
To foster our people's ongoing spiritual growth we have: • a how-to-pray course at least once a year; • a bookstall operating after most Sunday services and perhaps at other times; • regular book reviews from the pulpit and/or in the church bulletin; • a church library (with books, audio- and perhaps video-cassettes) in regular use by at least a significant minority of our people; • at least two courses on Bible study or theological topics a year; • at least one seminar per year on life-related themes; • a habit of regularly circulating photocopied articles particularly to leaders; • announcements at least twice a month of outside conventions or training opportunities for our people; • at least a significant minority of our young people attending Christian camps, Scripture Union beach missions, Christian groups at their schools or colleges and similar functions; • leadership training opportunities in

place for small group facilitators. (1) We would have at least five of the above in place (2) four (3) three (4) two (5) one or none.

14. Organisation
In our church's structure, • we have regular communication between the leaders and the church; • we open positions for junior members to join important leadership groups; • our leaders invite and receive regular written communications from church members; • we have a feedback mechanism which produces ideas and suggestions from many in the church; • we have a 'sabbatical' system so that leaders must retire for at least a year every six-to-eight years; • at least 30% of regular Sunday attenders would belong to a committee or task force during a two-year period. (1) We have all this in place (2) we have three of the above (3) two (4) one (5) none.

How did you score? If your total circled numbers was 14 (honest?) go straight to heaven: you have fulfilled your ministry! 15–20: your church is quite unique (but don't rush into organising seminars on 'how we succeed around here'!). 21–30 — excellent: now work on setting goals to improve. 31–40 — get the World Vision video 'Your Church Can Come Alive'. 41–50 — get the World Vision video and insist your leaders read one book each about church organisation and health. 51–60 — definitely get the video and get other churches in your area to combine for a live seminar with a consultant/facilitator. 61+ Don't get discouraged, and do all of the above!